Table of Contents

VEGAN DIET FOR ATHLETES

INTRODUCTION

COPYRIGHT © 2020 - ANDREA'S VEGAN DIET GUIDE

CHAPTER 1: WHAT IS A VEGAN DIET
- GETTING STARTED ON A VEGAN DIET
  - *Decide What a Vegan Diet Means for You*
  - *Understand What You Are Eating*
  - *Find Revamped Versions of Your Favorite Recipes*
  - *Build a Support Network*

CHAPTER 2: BENEFITS OF VEGAN DIET
- LOWERS BLOOD PRESSURE
- LOWERS CHOLESTEROL LEVEL
- MAINTAINS HEALTHY SKIN
- BOOSTS YOUR ENERGY
- LOWERS BLOOD SUGAR LEVELS
- ENHANCES YOUR DIGESTION
- PREVENTS CHRONIC DISEASES
  - *Cardiac Conditions*
  - *Cancer*
  - *Cognitive Decline*
  - *Diabetes*
- SAVES TIME AND MONEY
- FASTER RECOVERY AFTER WORKOUTS
- MORE ECO-FRIENDLY DIET

CHAPTER 3: HOW TO BALANCE PROPER NUTRITION COUNT
- WHAT TO EAT
- WHAT TO AVOID
  - *Calorie Intake*
  - *Nutrient Density*
  - *Macro Breakdown*
  - *Vegan Protein*
  - *Keep Variety in Your Diet*
  - *Create goals that you can reach.*
- SIMPLE NUTRITION EQUALS MORE MUSCLES

CHAPTER 4: WHAT TO EAT AND WHAT TO AVOID
- FOOD TO EAT
- WHAT TO AVOID
  - *Processed Foods*
  - *Unrefined Grains*
  - *Sugars*
- HOW TO REALLY EAT CLEAN
  - *Look at the nutrients, and not just the calories.*
  - *Move past refined white flours.*

- *Balance out your diet.*
- *Consume more water.*
- *Get plenty of fresh produce.*
- *Look at your meals as if it's a lifestyle.*

ENERGY-BOOSTING FOODS
- *Sweet Potatoes*
- *Coconut Oil*
- *Bananas*
- *Rolled Oats*
- *Walnuts*
- *Lentils*
- *Spinach*
- *Oranges*
- *Avocados*
- *Apricots*

CHAPTER 5: HOW VEGAN DIET HELPS TO GAIN STRENGTH
PLANNING A PROPER VEGAN MEAL
THE INFLUENCE OF VEGAN DIET ON ATHLETIC PERFORMANCE
PLANT BASED ANTIOXIDANTS VS ANTIOXIDANT SUPPLEMENTS
THE POSITIVE EFFECT OF VEGAN DIETS ON ATHLETIC SUCCESS
CALORIE AND PROTEIN REQUIREMENTS
PROTEIN REQUIREMENTS FOR VEGAN ATHLETES
- *Potential Dangers of Excess Proteins*

MUSCLE GROWTH

CHAPTER 6: 30 DAYS MEAL PLAN
WEEK 1
WEEK 2
WEEK 3
WEEK 4

CHAPTER 7: SHOPPING LIST
WEEK 1: SHOPPING LIST
WEEK 2: SHOPPING LIST
WEEK 3: SHOPPING LIST
WEEK 4: SHOPPING LIST

CHAPTER 8: BREAKFAST RECIPES
1. CHOCOLATE-ALMOND BUTTER SHAKE
2. SAVORY TEMPEH SANDWICHES
3. PROTEIN PANCAKES
4. COUSCOUS AND CHICKPEA BOWLS
5. BERRIES WITH MASCARPONE ON TOASTED BREAD
6. OVERNIGHT CHIA OATS
7. MEXICAN BREAKFAST
8. AMARANTH QUINOA PORRIDGE
9. CACAO LENTIL MUFFINS

10. Chickpea Crepes with Mushrooms and Spinach
11. Goji Breakfast Bowl
12. Breakfast Berry Parfait
13. Mini Tofu Frittatas
14. Brownie Pancakes
15. Fig & Cheese Oatmeal
15. Roasted Cauliflower Salad
16. Mediterranean Salad
17. Sweet and Smoky BBQ Salad
18. Vegetarian Taco Salad
19. Roasted Chickpea Gyros
20. Portobello Tofu Fajitas

CHAPTER 9: LUNCH RECIPES
21. Tofu and Veggies Buddha Bowl
22. Vegan Sheet Pan 3 Style Tofu
23. Buffalo Chickpeas and Lettuce Wraps
24. Lentil and Cheese Nuggets
25. Black Bean and Sweet Potato Burritos
26. Mac and Peas and Cashew Sauce
27. Chickpea, Mango and Curried Cauliflower Salad
28. Vegetable and Tofu Skewers
29. Baked deep-dish apple pancake
30. Black Bean and Veggie Soup
31. Spinach Pasta in Pesto Sauce
32. Vegan Alfredo Fettuccine Pasta
33. Tempeh Vegetarian Chili
34. Healthy Lentil Soup
35. Lentil Vegan Soup
36. Chickpea and Avocado Salad
37. Roasted Vegetables and Lentil Salad
38. Quinoa Salad Southwestern Style
39. Easy bean burritos
40. Sweet Potato, Spinach & Butter Bean Stew

CHAPTER 10: SOUP RECIPES
41. Tofu and mushroom soup
42. Avocado green soup
43. Spicy Black Bean Soup
44. Red Curry Quinoa Soup
45. Split Pea Soup
46. Tofu Noodle Soup
47. Hot and Sour Soup
48. Spicy SunDried Tomato Soup with White Beans & Swiss Chard
49. Lentil Spinach Soup
50. Potato, Bean and Kale Soup

CHAPTER 11: SALAD RECIPES
- 51. Mexican Street Salad
- 52. Mediterranean Bean Salad
- 53. Strawberry Spinach Salad with Avocado & Walnuts
- 54. Black Bean and Corn Salad
- 55. Pineapple & Avocado Salad
- 56. Edamame and Chickpeas Salad
- 57. Black and White Bean Quinoa Salad
- 58. Tempeh Salad
- 59. Edamame Salad
- 60. White bean and tomato salad
- 61. Tofu Bean Salad
- 62. Quinoa Salad
- 63. Thai Zucchini Noodle Salad
- 64. Bacon & Broccoli Salad
- 65. Green Curry Tofu
- 66. Fruit Salad
- 67. Berry salad with Arugula
- 68. Grilled tempeh and chickpea salad
- 69. Zucchini fennel salad
- 70. Vegan Greek salad

CHAPTER 12: DINNER RECIPES
- 71. Vegan Greek Meatball Soup
- 72. Irish "Lamb" Stew
- 73. Cauliflower Fried Rice
- 74. Sesame Tofu Veggies
- 75. Red Curry Mac and Cheese
- 76. Cauliflower Steaks
- 77. Tempeh Burgers
- 78. Butternut Squash Tofu Jambalaya
- 79. Vegan High Protein Chili
- 80. Vegan Chili for Sore Muscles
- 81. Tofu & Snow Pea Stir-Fry with Peanut Sauce
- 82. Crunchy Chickpea, Broccoli and Cheese Casserole
- 83. Teriyaki Tofu and Tempeh Casserole
- 84. Tomato & Garlic Butter Beans
- 85. Cheesy, Garlicky Pull Apart Pizza Bread
- 86. Baked BBQ Tofu with Caramelized Onions
- 87. Vegan Risotto with Sun Dried Tomatoes
- 88. Quinoa with Peas and Onion
- 89. Swiss chard with Onions & Garlic
- 90. Steamed Eggplants with Peanut Dressing

CONCLUSION

Introduction

Veganism is steadily gaining in popularity these days as the awareness about leading environment-friendly lifestyles is increasing. Along with its popularity, the general misconceptions about this diet are rising as well. All these widespread misconceptions have managed to trigger a somewhat restrictive and negative attitude toward veganism. These misconceptions are the only reason why a lot of people hesitate before transitioning to veganism. Going vegan might seem like a fad, but it is the best way to lead an environmentally conscious life.

This book contains proven steps and strategies on how to harness the power of a vegan diet. It will discuss what a vegan diet is, how to become vegan, the most popular reasons to become a vegan, famous athletes who are proudly vegan, and also talk about some of the supplements that are available for vegans.

If you would like to try the vegan lifestyle, you need to get it right from the start. Many people have given it a go but never really got to grips with it. To be honest, it is never easy because there isn't really a great deal of support around. But just like anything worth doing, stick at it and the results will come.

For those athletes who have successfully adopted the vegan ways, they have noticed some great benefits. One of those is that the body recovers quicker between training sessions. As you can imagine, if the athlete has a faster recovery, they can train more often and see quicker improvements. It's not the increased amount of training that is the best thing, it's the faster recovery that allows for the additional training. That's important.

Veganism is the new buzzword all over the world, with health fanatics steadily moving to a vegan diet for purported health advantage and the ethics about the treatment of animals. It has not only got the general population to take to this new form of living but also many athletes, sportsmen, and bodybuilders. However, to get the same amount of proteins from the plant-based diet as from animal diet is quite severe. Hence, it requires a measured form of eating the right proteins and in proper quantities in order to extract maximum protein. It is of paramount importance to athletes and bodybuilders as a lot of energy and calories are burned in physical activity and, thus need to be replaced with good proteins to get the desired effects.

Vegan bodybuilding for beginners can be tough but not impossible. It is undoubtedly a herculean task to get proteins from a plant-based diet, but there are ways and means to build up muscle for vegans. Let's find out how!

Anyone interested in bodybuilding requires large doses of protein to develop muscles. Reaching the protein goals while removing dairy and meat from the diet might not sound plausible. However, a vegan diet doesn't need to hold you back. You can attain all the protein your body needs without ever worrying about compromising the health of your muscles or your body in general.

This book is about using a vegan diet as fuel to live a more athletic lifestyle. You need to eat daily, so why not eat fibrous, nutritious, and plant-load your meals? I genuinely believe that with the information contained in this book, together with a keen interest in athletic living, you can learn that it is not difficult to eat a vegan diet and that anyone can take a vegan diet at any level. Now, if you are ready to learn more, then let us get started without further ado!

Chapter 1: What Is a Vegan Diet

Veganism is one type of a vegetarian diet. Exclusions for those who are vegan include any meat, dairy products, eggs, and any other ingredients that are derived from animals. A growing number of people who follow a vegan diet also do not eat any type of food that has been processed using any kind of animal products, including certain types of wines and white sugar that has been refined. The actual term "vegan" can either refer to the diet itself or a person who has adopted this style of eating.

To those who are not familiar with Veganism, this is the most common question that is asked. Many people have visions of a plate of salad night after night for the rest of their lives. In reality, a vegan diet is quite diverse. It includes fruits, vegetables, legumes, beans, and all grains. Think of the infinite combination of delicious meals that can be made from these ingredients! There are also vegan options for most of the popular dishes people enjoy eating. Some common examples include vegan mayonnaise, vegan cheese, vegan ice cream, vegan hot dogs, vegan pizza, and tons of others.

If you were to ask a vegan if they feel restricted by choosing to follow their diet, their answer would always be a resounding, "No".

Once you have made the decision to become a vegan, it can be difficult to know where to start. Do you shun all animal related products right away? Do you ease into it gently? The simple answer is that it will completely depend on you. While some people may find the switch a simple matter, others may struggle with their decision.

For people who find the commitment difficult in the beginning, one painless way to start is by becoming a vegetarian first. Once you have the basics of vegetarianism down pat, slowly omit dairy and eggs. There is no wrong or right way to go about becoming a vegan so do what feels right for you. In order to keep yourself on the right track, keep the reasons that you chose to become vegan in mind in the first place and the goals that you have set for yourself.

Many people do it; many people talk about it, but there is still a lot of confusion about what a vegan diet actually entails. Because we separate food into their macronutrients: sugars, carbohydrates, and fats, it is most times unclear to most of us. What if we could reassemble these macronutrients to free your mind from doubt and stress? Simplicity is the key here.

Whole foods are unprocessed foods that come from the soil. Today we eat some minimally processed foods such as fresh rice, whole wheat pasta, tofu, nondairy milk, and some nuts and seed butter on a whole food vegan diet. All of this is fine as long as it is done to a minimum. So, here are the different categories:

- Legumes (basically lentils and beans) of whole grains.
- Fruits and vegetables
- Nuts and seeds (including nut butter)
- Herbs and spices

All of the above categories constitute a whole vegan diet. How to prepare them is where it is fun; how to season and cook them; and how to mix and match to give them great taste and versatility in your meals. So long as you eat these things daily, you will forget about calories, carbohydrates, and fat forever.

Some of the benefits associated with vegan diets include:

- Lower risk of getting heart related disease
- Lower cholesterol levels as well as low density lipoprotein
- Lower blood pressure
- Lower chances of getting type 2 diabetes
- Lower risk of cancer
- Lower BMI

It is important to note that all these benefits are not acquired just by avoiding animal products like meat. The high consumption of whole foods like whole grains, beans, nuts, seeds, fruits and vegetables which contain beneficial nutrients, vitamins, minerals, antioxidants as well as phytochemicals is what is responsible for all these health gains.

The truth is that most animal products as well as processed foods which consist of 90% of the calories in the average Americans diet do not contain good phytochemicals or antioxidants which are usually found in unrefined plant based foods.

A vegan diet always raises questions regarding it's ability to supply micronutrients to the body. How well these questions are grounded depends a lot on the composition of the diet. Most vegan diets comprising high refined carbohydrate content and little amounts of whole plant foods will easily lack in essential micronutrients. Therefore, vegan athletes need to eat foods that are rich in the following nutrients, fats, and minerals.

- Omega 3 essential fats
- Minerals like calcium, zinc, iodine, and iron
- Vitamins B12 and D
- Sources of calcium and iron in the vegan diet
- Calcium

Exercise leads to depletion of iron reserves putting athletes at risk of iron deficiency. Professional female athletes are at high risk of iron depletion and anemia according to studies.

In most cases an iron rich diet is important in the needs of a female vegan athlete. However, supplementation might be necessary in special cases such as anemia and iron depletion due to heavy menstruation.

Iron levels in the body should be kept at optimum. High amounts of iron have been linked to cardiovascular conditions and even increase risk of heart attack. For men, the low recommended daily intake of iron can be achieved through eating green leafy vegetables. However, the amount of green leafy vegetables consumed daily should be large enough to ensure that the body gets a good amount of this mineral. If this is not possible, there are other suggestions for great sources of iron which I mention later.

Getting started on a vegan diet

Common misunderstandings among many people—even in the health and fitness industry is that anyone who switches to a vegan diet will automatically become super healthy. There are plenty of vegan junk foods out there, such as frozen veggie pizza and nondairy ice cream, which can really kill your health goals if you eat them all the time. Engaging in healthy foods is the only way you can reap health benefits.

On the other side, certain vegan snacks play a role in keeping you focused.

They should be consumed in moderation, sparingly and in small bits.

Decide What a Vegan Diet Means for You

The first step is to make a determination on how to organize your vegan diet to help you move from your present culinary viewpoint. This is really unique, something that ranges from individual to individual. While some people choose not to consume any animal products at all, others make do with tiny bits of dairy or food at times. It really is up to you to decide what and how you want your vegan diet to look like. Perhaps notably, you have to make a large portion of your diet from whole vegan foods.

Understand What You Are Eating

Okay, now that you've made the decision, your next move on your side part requires a lot of study. What do we mean by that? Okay, if this is your first time trying out the vegan diet, the amount of foods containing animal products, particularly packaged foods, will shock you. You will find yourself cultivating the custom of reading tags when shopping. It points out that many pre-packaged foods contain animal products, and you need to keep a close eye on the packaging of the ingredients if you just want to stick to plant products for your new diet. You may have decided to allow a certain number of animal products in your diet; well, you'll just have to look out for foods filled with fats, carbohydrates, salt, preservatives, and other things that may affect your healthy diet.

Find Revamped Versions of Your Favorite Recipes

I'm sure you have plenty of favorite dishes, not necessarily vegan. For most people, leaving everything behind is usually the most difficult part. Nonetheless, there is still a way to meet you halfway. Take some time to think about those things you want that are not based on plants. Think along the lines of taste, shape, consistency, and so on; and search for substitutes throughout the diet based on food plants that can do what you're lacking.

Build a Support Network

Building a new routine is complicated, but it doesn't have to be. Find some friends that are glad to be with you in this lifestyle, or even family members. This will help you stay focused and motivated by having a form of emotional support and openness. You can do fun things like try out and share new recipes with these mates or even hit up restaurants offering a variety of vegan options. You can even go one step further and look up local vegan social media groups to help you expand your knowledge and support network.

Chapter 2: Benefits of Vegan Diet

Lowers Blood Pressure

The plant-based diet is known to lower blood pressure. This is due to the fact that the plant-based diet has very little amounts of sugars, which aid in raising the blood pressure. If you have a condition of high blood pressure, a plant-based diet is the right remedy for you.

Lowers Cholesterol Level

Let me start by asking you a question; how much do you think one egg affects your cholesterol? One egg a day could increase your dietary cholesterol from 97 to 418 mg in a single day! There was a study done on seventeen lacto-vegetarian college students. During this study, the students were asked to consume 400kcal in test foods along with one large egg for three weeks. During this time, their dietary cholesterol raised to these numbers. To put it in perspective, 200 to 239 mg/dL is considered borderline high.

Maintains Healthy Skin

We all know people who try every skin product imaginable just to get clear, smooth skin. What these people fail to understand is that how we look is more or less dictated by our food choices. Consequently, plant-based diets have a higher chance of providing your skin with the nutrients it needs to stay healthy. For instance, tomatoes provide the body with lycopene. This component safeguards the skin from sun damage. Sweet potatoes are known to provide us with vitamin C. The production of collagen will help your skin glow and encourage fast healing.

Boosts Your Energy

Minerals and vitamins are good sources of energy for the body. Plants are not only rich in them, but also contain phytonutrients, antioxidants, proteins, and healthy fats. All of these are essential nutrients for your brain. In addition, they are easy to digest, which makes it easy for the body to obtain energy from them.

Lowers Blood Sugar Levels

The plant-based diet has little or no sugars at all. Most non-plant diets are known to contain high levels of sugars. This, in turn, causes diabetes. A plant-based diet lowers the level of blood sugar thereby making it healthy for your body.

Enhances Your Digestion

Good digestion calls for plenty of fiber. The good news is that plants offer sufficient fiber to facilitate good digestion. It is vital to understand that you cannot just start eating tons of vegetables and fruits without a plan. If you are starting this diet, you should start slow. Your body needs ample time to adjust. Therefore, you should introduce your new diet slowly to prevent constipation, since most of it is composed of fiber.

Prevents Chronic Diseases

Besides aiding in weight loss, a whole-food plant-based diet has also been proven to help lower the risks of various chronic health conditions.

Cardiac Conditions

This is the most widely-known benefit of whole-food plant-based diets as they have higher probabilities of keeping your cardiac health sound. But, the strength of this benefit is dependent on the types and quality of the food in your diet plan. Major research done on over 200,000 people concluded that the risk of having heart disease was lower in those people whose diet plan was plant-based and was rich in whole grains, veggies, nuts, legumes, and fruits than those who were following non-plant-based diets.

But, plant-based diet plans that are unhealthy because of the inclusion of fruit juices, refined grains, and sugary drinks showed an increased risk of cardiac complications. This is why it is very important to stick to the right foods and follow a healthy plant-based diet plan.

Cancer

According to various research studies, a plant-based diet plan can lower the risks of various forms of cancer. A study of over 69,000 people found that the risk of gastrointestinal cancer was very low for vegetarian diet followers, especially for Lacto-ovo vegetarian diet followers (the ones who consume both dairy and eggs).

In another study of over 77,000 people, it was proven that there was a 22 percent reduced risk of having colorectal cancer in those who followed a vegetarian diet plan than those who didn't. The safest was pescatarians (those vegetarians who consume fish) as they had a significant 43 percent lower risk of colorectal cancer than non-vegetarian diet plan followers.

Cognitive Decline

Various studies found that diet plans high in fruit and veggie content can prevent or slow Alzheimer's disease and cognitive decline in adults. The reason is that many foods in plant-based diet plans are high in antioxidants and plant compounds that act as protective agents against the development of Alzheimer's disease and reversing cognitive damage.

A review of nine research studies of around 31,000 people found that those who consumed more veggies and fruits had a significant 20 percent lower risk of having dementia or cognitive impairment.

Diabetes

A whole-food plant-based diet plan can play a significant role in lowering the risk of contracting diabetes or managing the illness. In a study involving over 200,000 people, it was proven that there was a 34 percent reduced risk of having diabetes if you followed a healthy, plant-based diet in comparison to an unhealthy, non-plant-based plan.

In another research study, it was proven that both Lacto-ovo vegetarian and vegan diet plans could lower the risk of type 2 diabetes by a whopping 50 percent in comparison to non-plant-based diet plans. Plant-based diet plans are also known to cause improvements in blood sugar level control in people with diabetes as compared to non-plant-based diets.

Saves Time and Money

A plant-based diet is generally known to be cheaper compared to a non-plant diet such as meat. When it also comes to cooking, a plant-based diet takes less time to be ready thereby saving you some valuable time which you can use to do other things.

Faster Recovery After Workouts

Athletes, runners, and bodybuilders on plant-based diets report that they recover faster after workouts, meaning they can fit in more training than their omnivorous counterparts. This may be due to increased antioxidants, vitamins, potassium, or a decrease in the inflammatory compounds found in meat and dairy.

More Eco-Friendly Diet

The whole-food plant-based diet plan is not only beneficial in terms of health but also proven to be better for the ecosystem. Plant-based diet plan followers tend to have a smaller effect on the environment in comparison to other diet plan followers.

Sustainable eating approaches can help lower greenhouse gas effects as well as land and water consumption required for factory farming. These factors are known to be the major cause of harm to the ecosystem and global warming.

Chapter 3: How to balance proper Nutrition Count

What to Eat

Here's a quick list of the foods that you should eat more of when you're on a plant-based diet program:

- Fruits – Berries, citrus fruits, apples, bananas, grapes, avocados, melons, dates, cantaloupe, apricots, cranberries, coconut, figs, guava, plums, kiwi, papaya, pears, pomelo, watermelon
- Vegetables – Beetroot, broccoli, cauliflower, kale, carrots, potatoes, tomatoes, asparagus, red bell peppers, onions, garlic, ginger, zucchini, spinach, sweet potatoes, butternut squash, green beans
- Legumes – Lentils, peas, chickpeas, kidney beans, black beans, navy beans, pinto beans, peanuts
- Nuts – Almonds, walnuts, pistachios, hazel nuts, Brazilian nuts, cashews, pecans, macadamia,
- Seeds – Pumpkin seeds, chia seeds, flaxseeds, sunflower seeds, hemp seeds
- Healthy oils – Olive oil, vegetable oil, avocado oil, flaxseed oil
- Whole grains – Oats, brown rice, barley, quinoa, whole wheat bread, rye, buckwheat, spelt, cornmeal
- Plant-based milk – Almond milk, soy milk, coconut milk, oat milk, rice milk, hemp milk
- Seasonings, herbs and spices – Salt, pepper, basil, rosemary, thyme, oregano, paprika, cumin, cinnamon
- Beverages – Water, fresh fruit juices, smoothies, vegetable shakes

Here are some foods that you can also eat but only occasionally:

- Meat – Beef, pork, lamb
- Seafood – Fish, shells, crabs, lobsters
- Poultry – Chicken, turkey, duck
- Dairy – Milk, butter, mayo, yogurt, cheese
- Other animal products – Eggs, honey

What to Avoid

As for the foods to avoid, here's a list of those that you should avoid as much as possible:

- Processed foods
- Sugary treats
- Refined white carbohydrates
- High-sodium, high-fat food products
- Soda
- Alcohol

Tips

To help make sure that you achieve success with this diet program, take note of the following tips:

- Write down your menu – Having a weekly menu eliminates the guesswork on what to prepare, and at the same time, helps you make use of your time more efficiently. When you're running late and don't know what to prepare for lunch or dinner, it's a lot easier to get tempted to go back to your old eating habits.
- Focus on dishes that you love – The great thing about the plant-based diet is not as strict as other diet plans. And because it's versatile, you can focus on consuming dishes that you actually enjoy so that the transition will not feel too much like a chore.
- Don't be too hard on yourself – Like any other diet program, the plant based meal prep takes time and effort. If you are not patient enough, you will not achieve the results that you want. Keep in mind that it's not something that can be achieved overnight.

Calorie Intake

While calorie counting is a touchy subject among many, some will argue that it is better that you don't do it, for bodybuilders, it plays a big part in their nutrition. When your goals are to add muscle mass, you have to make sure that your body has the fuel it needs to increase and build the size of the muscle fibers. And if you start reducing your calorie intake, you will start losing fat. This helps to make you look more muscular, even though you aren't gaining new muscle.

You have to know what your true calorie needs are. You can't guess, estimate, or assume things about your habits. You need to use real data that is based upon what you do and who you are.

Since not everybody is the same, you can't give a baseline number for how many calories you need to consume. But lucky for you, there are a lot of online calculators that can do the math for you. Head over to bodybuilding.com and use their online calculator to figure out how many calories you should be aiming for during your different phases.

Nutrient Density

Nutrient density of food refers to how many nutrients you will get from it, given how many calories it has. Nutrients are what provide your body with nourishment, energy, muscle recovery, allows for growth, and maintains life. Think about phytonutrients, nitric oxide, water, fiber, antioxidants, amino acids, minerals, and vitamins. If you want to go for foods with lots of nutrients, then you will want to aim for whole foods.

If you think about it, whole foods don't contain anything that shouldn't be there. There is a big difference between eating 2500 calories of plant foods like seeds, nuts, grains, veggies, and fruits and eating 2500 calories of ice cream, candy, pizza, and friends. You're getting 2500 calories both ways, but only one of them will provide you with all of the necessary nutrients that you need.

That means low-calorie, nutrient-dense foods are going to give you bigger rewards than foods that are high in calories, cut contain few nutrients. If you eat a high-calorie, nutrient-poor diet, you are going to struggle to reach your fitness goals, no matter what those goals may be.

Macro Breakdown

A big mistake that people will make when they start following a vegan bodybuilding diet is that they forget to eat enough good calories, which can end up hurting the muscle-building goals. To make sure you are getting quality calories, you will need to know its macro breakdown.

Macronutrients, as mentioned before, are fat, carbohydrates, and protein. They are all major nutrients that your body has to have in order to function efficiently and properly. Counting your macros simply ensures that you consume a certain balance of each macro every day. Following a macro diet is also considered a flexible diet because you are allowed to consume whatever you want as long as you hit your numbers.

And guess what? This breakdown is the same for vegans and meat-eaters alike. The amount of macronutrients you need to consume is going to remain the same. The only difference is you will use vegan foods to reach it. There aren't any hard-and-fast rules as to what your macro breakdown needs to be, and your ratios will probably change depending on where competition day is sitting. For bodybuilders, you typically want to keep your carbs up, fats moderate, and protein high enough to help support the growth of muscle. Then you will typically cut that right before a competition by decreasing your carb intake a lot and your fat intake slightly.

Vegan Protein

There are a lot of different vegan protein sources out there, more than people know. You have hemp seeds, vital wheat gluten, fava beans, seitan, tempeh, bean pasta, textured vegetable protein, tofu, and lupini beans, just to name a few.

There is also vegan protein powder that you can use in place of whey protein in smoothies, and research has found that it is just as effective as whey protein. Oatmeal, black beans, kidney beans, nuts, nut butters, and amaranth are other great protein options for vegans. And there are even some foods that you wouldn't think contains protein that does, such as Brussels sprouts, mushrooms, chlorella, greens, and potatoes.

Keep Variety in Your Diet

When it comes to meal-prepping and counting calories and macros, it may be very tempting to eat the same things over and over again. But to make any meal plan good, whether you're vegan or not, is to make sure it has a lot of variety.

When you have variety in your diet, you will be getting all of the micronutrients you need, and you will be consuming all of the amino acids your body will need. This is especially true during your "cutting" period. This is when poor meal planning can end up causing nutritional deficiencies.

Yes, you can absolutely be a vegan bodybuilder while also gaining muscle and losing fat. And if you need a bit of inspiration, you can also turn to Instagram to see what others are doing.

Create goals that you can reach.

Document all of your workouts so that you can hold yourself accountable.

You want to train consistently and keep a level of intensity that is going to elicit and ignite change.

It is important that you track your workouts along with your food. While this may seem like a waste of time, or super tedious, it will be worth it in the long run. Things will become second nature. And you may find that meal tracking is the secret to reaching all of your bodybuilding goals. You have the tools you need, so now you just have to do it.

Simple Nutrition Equals More Muscles

If you were a plant-based bodybuilder a decade ago, you would have been seen as an oxymoron. For a long time now, all we have heard is that in order to build muscles, you have to eat a lot of meat. The times are changing, and bodybuilders now realize that they don't want to consume as many animal products.

It's obvious that a plant-based diet can provide you with lots of health benefits. People who follow a plant-based diet have a lower risk of obesity than the national average. Considering that there is research that says processed and red meat can shorten a person's life expectancies, plant-based dieters tend to live longer.

But, there is still concern among bodybuilders about the ability to increase or maintain their size and strength. I want to assure you that when you start taking into account the attention and planning that you put into your lifestyle, you will quickly realize that being a vegan bodybuilder isn't all that much harder to follow than the diet you are following right now.

There are bodybuilding nutrition facts that remain true even if you are following a plant-based diet. The truth is, all you are doing is adapting what you have already learned about building muscle and getting rid of fat and turning it plant-based. You are simply making your nutrition simpler.

There are few important pieces of information to take into consideration when you switch to a plant-based diet as a bodybuilder. This includes making sure you get enough protein, you keep your carbs balanced, along with plenty of vitamin B12, EPA, and DHA.

Chapter 4: What to Eat and What to Avoid

The vegan diet is believed to be amongst the most popular diets these days. Going vegan is not just a diet, but is more of a lifestyle choice that actively eliminates different forms of animal cruelty for the sake of meeting the demands of human beings for clothing, food, or enjoyment. There are various reasons why people embrace veganism. Maybe you want to opt for veganism because it helps improve your overall health, endorses ethical treatment of animals, or merely because it is more environmentally conscious. Regardless of the reasons for opting for a vegan diet, it is amongst the best diets today. You can easily attain your fitness and bodybuilding goals while choosing veganism.

Opting for a vegan diet can help reduce the risk of type II diabetes, along with different heart diseases. A vegan diet is also believed to help improve the health of your kidneys. Apart from this, it increases the presence of high-density lipoprotein (HDL) in your body. This cholesterol molecule is beneficial and helps reduce the risk of different cardiovascular diseases. It also helps tackle and regulate inflammation. There are various health benefits you can reap by following a vegan lifestyle. You can do all this while being environmentally conscious. A vegan diet is rich in fiber and nutrients that your body needs. Therefore, by consuming hearty vegan meals, you improve the energy levels in your body.

Food to eat

A vegan diet is quite nourishing and rich in wholesome foods. Without exceeding your daily calorie intake, you can provide your body with all the nutrients and fiber it needs. So, if you want a lean physique, then the vegan diet works well. However, it doesn't mean you cannot bulk up while following a vegan diet. All that you need to do is be mindful of the proteins you consume.

A vegan bodybuilding diet usually includes the following foods.

- Beans and legumes are a great source of protein, as well as dietary fibers.
- Hemp seeds, sunflower seeds, and Chia seeds, and flaxseeds are not only rich in protein, but also omega-3 fatty acids.
- Soy products like tofu, tempeh, soy milk, soy protein powder, and edamame.
- To meet your daily requirement for vitamin D as well as calcium, start

adding calcium-fortified plant-based milk and yogurts.
- Whey isn't the only protein powder you can consume. With the increasing popularity of veganism, there are different vegan protein powders available in the market. According to your exercise and nutritional needs, you can select a protein powder.
- Nutritional yeast, as well as spirulina, are rich in vitamins and minerals.
- Whole grains and cereals, along with oats and other sprouted grain bread, are an excellent source of protein, as well as complex carbs.
- All fruits and vegetables are included.
- Different nuts, as well as nut-based butter, are rich in unhealthy fats as well as proteins.
- Healthy vegan condiments like hummus and tahini are a great way to sneak in healthy fats along with protein.
- Start using healthy oils like olive oil, hemp seed oil, and avocado oil for cooking. These oils are a rich source of healthy Omega-3 fatty acids.
- There are different meat substitutes you can add to your diet that are rich in protein but are made of soy or pea proteins.
- Two superfoods you can start adding to your diet are quinoa and amaranth.

So, there are plenty of protein sources you can easily include in your diet while staying true to veganism. You don't have to depend on animal-based nutrition to meet your body's protein requirements. Apart from this, you can consult with your doctor and start taking any dietary supplements you might require. Taking away the multi-vitamins and along with a vegan protein powder can help ensure that your body gets all the protein it requires while staying well within your calorie limit.

What to avoid

Processed Foods

One of the most popular pieces of advice you will receive about clean eating says that if it's processed, it can't be clean. Basically, if something comes prepackaged and is located within those horrible "middle aisles" of the grocery store, then you should run far and fast away from it. Most clean eating people will slap those boxes right out of your hand.

Processing foods isn't all that bad, and it often improve its safety and bioavailability of some antioxidants and nutrients. It also gives you the chance to quickly fix all of the lovely and delicious dishes on Instagram and

Pinterest.

Plus, there are plenty of healthy processed foods out there, such as hummus, whole-grain cereal, tomato sauce. Nutrition is a very complex subject, and sure it might be easier if we could just wipe out complete categories of food, but all this does is hurt your taste buds, wallet, and time.

Unrefined Grains

Unlike the processed food advice, the people who say unrefined grains are better than refined grains are right. Whole grains are a great way to consume fiber, and they have a lot of B vitamins. Refined grains get around 20 various nutrients taken out of them, but then most of them added back in during processing. But there is a caveat; there are a lot of grains that don't add back the important nutrients. If at all possible, go with the unrefined grains to make sure you get all of the nutrients they have to offer.

Sugars

There are some who even include fat and salt into this, but I won't get into how this is such an outdated way of thinking. Foods that have added sugars are pretty much useless, especially for non-athletes. If you are a bodybuilder training for competition, then some added sugars aren't going to hurt you. Sugars, when added to foods in order to make them more palatable, as opposed to the sugars that come natural in some foods, only add calories with no real health benefits.

How to Really Eat Clean

Getting clean shouldn't require a huge overhaul to your diet, especially if you are switching to a plant-based diet. If you go at it that way, then you are probably going about it wrong. Here are some things to keep in mind when getting clean.

Look at the nutrients, and not just the calories.

Don't allow yourself to get caught up in the numbers. When it comes to our bodyweight-conscious world, it's very easy to get caught in the numbers game. While it might work well for a person looking to lose weight, it isn't going to actually make them healthy.

The calorie-counting diet dates back to the 70s and 80s and is a thing of the past. It is much more important that you get all of the nutrients you need to than to focus on your overall calorie balance. Look at it this way; one way will make you feel grumpy and guilty when you do eat. The other gives you energy, stabilizes your blood sugar, and you will discover foods you never knew existed.

Move past refined white flours.

You can cut out the refined white flours you use for baking, and bake some things with unrefined flours and other flour substitutes. It could mean that you have to try out some new recipes and make some mistakes, but it is doable. Besides looking for unrefined wheat flours, you can also try out oat, brown rice, coconut, and almond flour. Using those choices will help to lower your carbohydrate intake, and you can still make delicious dishes with them.

These various flours also come with different nutritional profiles, so you will want to read on them to see which one fits your dietary needs the most.

Balance out your diet.

The two main ideas of clean eating are moderation and balance. You shouldn't avoid dietary fats and carbs completely, or you are going to end up dreading mealtimes. Make sure you eat them, but simply adjust your portion sizes so that it fits into your goals and nutrient needs.

Depending on your system needs, your macro ratio could end up being broken down into several different ways. If you lean more towards unsaturated fats and complex carbohydrates, then you are on the right track. What it all boils down to is to make sure that you are mindful of the foods you eat. You have a problem when you don't know what you are consuming.

Consume more water.

If you can't handle straight water all day long to get in your daily goals, then you can experiment with some other drinks, such as herbal or green tea. You can also flavor your water with lemon, or you can mix in sugar-free electrolytes. You can also have coffee, but if you're serious about being clean, it has to be black and not of that stuff that comes in a fancy cup.

Get plenty of fresh produce.

It doesn't matter what type of diet you're following; the golden rule of clean eating is to include as much fresh produce as you can. Vegetables make any diet healthier and better. They will give you nutrients and vitamins to help you feel as good as you look. It will also ensure that you have enough soluble fiber so that you can absorb all of the nutrition that you can get out of the food you eat.

You can't get all of those benefits from a supplement. That supplement will become an excuse you use so that you can cheat when you do get hungry. So make sure that you figure out your favorite fruits and veggies, and you can use the frozen ones if you need to. Also, don't be afraid to use spices and seasonings.

Look at your meals as if it's a lifestyle.

Eating clean isn't a diet you have to follow. It is simply a lifestyle that you will be able to sustain from here on out. You don't have to go off the deep end and start throwing out all of the food you love. You can enjoy your food, and you will need to do so in order to stick with this new lifestyle. And you may just have to push yourself so that you start cooking things yourself.

With these eight "rules" in mind, I am fully confident that you will be able to eat clean and enjoy the foods that have.

Energy-Boosting Foods

Sweet Potatoes

These tubers are a much better alternative to the white potato. They provide loads of minerals and vitamins, such as beta-carotene, manganese, vitamin C, and disease-preventing dietary fiber. These are a great choice for bodybuilders and athletes because when they are consumed in conjunction with protein after your workout, they act as a catalyst to help the protein move into your muscle tissue and start the repairing process.

Sweet potatoes are considered hypoallergenic and are one of the tops sources for post-workout carbs from most exercises, bodybuilders, and athletes who would like to up their energy but keep body fat down. A baked or steamed small to medium sweet potato can be a great post-workout snack.

Coconut Oil

This is a good fat full of "medium-chained" fats, which make it very easy to digest, as compared to other dietary fats. They are able to provide an easily accessible source of energy. Coconut oil is also a natural way to increase your metabolism, which gives your body the ability to burn more energy and boosts athletic performance. It also helps the function of the thyroid and gets rid of pancreatic stress, which will make you more active. You can easily add a couple of tablespoons into a smoothie.

Bananas

Bananas are a great source of potassium, which is an electrolyte that the body needs but loses when you are exercising. Appalachian State University did a study that found bananas were helpful in fueling cyclist during intense exercise. Bananas are also great at preventing muscle fatigue. Choosing a banana over an energy bar is much better options for some energy. They have a lot less sugar, and they have a lot more nutrients.

Rolled Oats

Oats are full of fiber, and they not only reduce your risk of developing heart disease, but they will also slow your glucose absorption, which will help to keep your energy up and your blood sugar levels steady. Oats also have a lot of B vitamins, which helps your body to change carbohydrates into usable energy.

Walnuts

Since you won't be getting your Omega-3s from fish, walnuts should be your go-to. They are a great way to get those heart-healthy omega-3 fatty acids. Good fats are a very important part of your diet if you are serious about achieving optimal health and fitness. Healthy fats are able to help heal your body from bruises, sprains, and other tissue injuries, as well as aid in energy production. Unhealthy fats, on the other hand, can slow you down. Have a can of walnuts with your at all times just encase you start feeling sluggish, or, if you make your own trail mix, add in some walnuts.

Lentils

Lentils are full of dietary fiber, containing eight grams in a half-cup serving. They are also great at keeping you feeling fuller for longer, and they will keep your energy levels up for your busy day.

Spinach

Spinach is full of folic acid and B vitamins, and both of these will provide you with lots of energy. Spinach can easily be added into different meals, from smoothies to scrambles and casseroles.

Oranges

If you need a quick boost of energy, oranges should be your go-to food. It is full of natural sugars, and they will also give you three grams of fiber, which can help to sustain your energy levels. A single navel orange will help you to meet your daily requirement for vitamin C.

Avocados

This delicious fruit is a great source of healthy fats that can activate your body. Your body can also utilize it for fuel to help you through your day or workout. It is also a great source of B6, folic acid, vitamin K, fiber, and vitamin C. Vitamin C is a great antioxidant that will help to support your adrenal glands, which you can end up overworking during stressful times. While B vitamins help with several functions within the body, they are often seen as the "stress and energy" vitamins. During a workout, your body becomes very stressed, so avocados work like a magic fruit.

Apricots

The last food on this list is apricots. There are some people who believe if they don't eat before a workout, they will end up burning more fat. While this may be true in some instances, it can also cause people to become dizzy, nausea, and lack important energy, which will hinder your ability to get the workout you want. Having a simple snack of an apricot before you workout can help give you the nutrients you need as well as an easily digested fuel to prevent all of those nasty side effects.

If you make sure you consume these energy-producing foods, along with others, you will never be lacking in energy or vitality. And, since you were a bodybuilder first, you should easily be able to slide into a plant-based diet that is full of these healthy energy-inducing foods without having to think about it.

Chapter 5: How Vegan Diet helps to gain strength

Since time immemorial bodybuilders have relied heavily on a high-meat and poultry diet to get the requisite amount of proteins to build muscle mass. However, there is a steady rise in the new wave of bodybuilders who are challenging the traditional norm of getting proteins only from meats and milk and instead are propagating plant-powered food. This new community of bodybuilders believes that with a strict commitment to a plant-based diet and a change in eating habits, one can get enough proteins for bodybuilding. Vegan bodybuilding diet can help in a great way to attain this goal. But before plunging into a full-fledged vegan diet, there are a few tips that can help get started with this regime-Get enough calories-The most important thing for new vegans is to take enough calories on a regular basis so that the body does not consume incoming protein for fueling body growth. This could lead to a deficit.

Have vegetables and fruits in plenty-It is important to take in a good quantity of fruits and vegetables as they keep up the nutrient content in the body and also provide antioxidants to maintain immunity.

Eat legumes and chickpeas-For vegans looking to build muscle, it is important to consume sufficient quantities of legumes and chickpeas. They are a high source of carbohydrates and make for a tasty snack after a rigorous session of workout.

Switch to quinoa instead of rice-Quinoa is a mixture of brown rice and oatmeal and is higher in the overall content of protein than brown rice. Also, it is a complete protein source, which is essential for muscle building.

Soy protein powder-Include soy protein powder with other natural sources of protein to increase the amount of protein in your body. In fact, it should be a must-have for all bodybuilders.

Avoid processed food-In vegan bodybuilding for beginners' diet, the consumption

of processed food is limited. Being vegan does not mean that you can have a free hand at eating any amounts of carbohydrates. Eating healthy is of prime importance with a diet containing nuts, fresh fruits, vegetables, and whole grains.

Have a short but intense workout-As a vegan, you should indulge in short, intense workouts. It will not allow the loss of muscle mass and will let your body rely on vegan protein sources through the workout sessions. It has been seen that long workout sessions often lead to fatigue for vegans in the long run.

Have a varied choice in food you consume-As a vegan, you might find yourselves eating the same food repeatedly. Try to avoid this as it can lead to nutritionally deficiencies and not add to muscle building.

Eat frequent meals-Since you can not consume as much protein in each meal as a non-vegetarian, you should add more meals to your day so that there is a steady stream of proteins going into the muscles.

Food rich in muscle-building amino acids-Amino acids are the building blocks of tissues and protein in the body. The body requires 21 amino acids to stay alive, and nine are found in food. These are called essential amino acids, and one of them called cinephile is related to muscle-building and it allows protein synthesis in the body through enzyme activation needed for cell growth. Thus, the leucine content in the meal shows the protein content required for muscle building. So eat foods rich in amino acids and especially leucine.

Making these simple lifestyle changes will go a long way in adjusting to the vegan way of life and will allow the proteins to be absorbed well to create as much muscle mass as a non-vegan diet would.

Planning a proper vegan meal

Meal planning is of the utmost importance when undertaking a vegan diet, especially for bodybuilders and athletes.

There are a few things that you need to keep in mind while planning a proper diet-Calorie Intake-Accurate calorie tracking is the most effective and reliable way to know what is going into the body, how to lose fat, and build muscle. It does not mean starving yourself, but instead, it includes the number of calories you eat and how many you might burn. It is called energy balance.

- Work out Macros-There are three macronutrients that the body needs-proteins, fats, and carbohydrates. They make up a major part of our calorie intake and the macronutrient split is essential to build a great looking body for bodybuilders. They dictate how the body will grow and repair tissues, and how much muscle you retain during a weight loss program. The optimal vegan macro split should be-Have a high-protein diet consuming 0.73-1 g per lbs.

- Plan meat timing and portions-Once you have figured out how to split the macronutrients in every meal, it is time to plan your meal timing and also the portion size. Since you are getting all the proteins from plants; it is not feasible to get the requisite amounts in just three main meals of the day. Hence, it is pertinent to add more meals at frequent intervals with substantial amounts of protein in each meal. It will help stoke the metabolic fire and burn more fat. In addition to it, the continuous consumption of protein will help in muscle growth at optimal capacity. The timing of the meal is also important. Late night dinners or might-night snacks are a big no. Stay away from food after sunset or reduce it to minimal.

- Plan what foods for each meal-It is important to decide on the kind of proteins you want to have in each meal. So planning each meal with care is significant. Include fresh fruits, nuts, and vegetables on a daily basis. Get the macronutrient split right so that there is a proper percentage of each nutrient for adequate muscle repair and growth.

The influence of vegan diet on athletic performance

Evidence has shown that many high performing professional and amateur athletes experience lower immune-competence (weakened immune systems). This is usually accompanied by frequent infection of the upper respiratory tract.

Such symptoms are usually the result of prolonged stress from regular high-intensity training. Similarly, a short period of intense exercise creates a temporary reduction in immune function. Some of the properties of the immune system reduced by high-intensity training include: *neutrophil function* and the natural cell degeneration number.

Intense workouts have a negative effect on the neutrophil function (white blood cells) and this can lead to poor immune-response and increase in microbial infections. Consequently, it will lead to a disruption in training and affect the athlete's performance. Coaches and trainers, who work with top professional and amateur athletes, usually want training to be continuous without any interruptions due to illness caused by viral infections. That is why it is beneficial for all dedicated athletes who adopt a vegan diet to choose foods that will effectively boost immune-competence. Thus, the athlete will be able to enjoy continuous training without disruptions due to illness.

Plant Based Antioxidants vs Antioxidant Supplements

A diet with relatively high quantity of phytochemicals (chemical compounds that occur naturally in plants) and antioxidants can also reduce oxidative stress caused by intense training. Just one bout of an intense workout can produce a significant amount of oxidative stress in the muscles and blood stream. This may stay on for a couple of days during which the endogenous antioxidant defenses are increased. On the contrary, reactive oxygen species (ROS) created by the intense workout may outweigh the increase in endogenous antioxidants. But regular consumption of high-antioxidant plant based foods keeps ROS at desirable levels and reduces the negative effects of oxidative stress.

But it is important to note that antioxidant supplements have not produced predictable results when used to reduce oxidative stress induced by intense training or to curtail inflammatory markers. In some cases, these supplements have actually slowed down recovery. In one study, creatine kinase, which is a major indicator of muscle damage, remained at a high level for a longer period than those who were given a placebo.

In a second study, administering a concentrated antioxidant to the participants raised lipid peroxidation and reduced the level of glutathione peroxidase – an antioxidant enzyme. Other reports and some studies of chronic diseases show that high micronutrient whole foods, which contain complex mixtures of phyto-nutrients and antioxidants, are more potent than supplements containing high doses of isolated antioxidants. There is also strong evidence showing that vegetables protect the body against coronary heart failure which also involves oxidative damage. But the benefit of using antioxidant vitamin supplements to prevent this disease is not clear.

Broccoli, collards, kale, bok choy and other green vegetables, provide a significantly higher quantity of micronutrients per kilocalorie than other foods. They also contain protein. Virtually all colorful vegetables are rich in antioxidants. In addition, fruits like kiwi, oranges, sour cherries, pomegranates, berries and black currants, have high quantities of antioxidants. Seeds like black unhulled sesame seed and pistachio nuts also have high amounts of antioxidants including vitamin E.

The Positive Effect of Vegan Diets on Athletic Success

In the American Journal of Clinical Nutrition, many reviews of successful athletes who ate vegan diets are documented. As far back the 1890s, vegan long distance walkers and cyclists in Britain and the U.S. performed better than those who ate meat. A vegan became one of the first athletes to finish the marathon race under two and a half hours, in 1912. In 1970, research conducted to compare pulmonary function and muscle width in athletes revealed that there was no difference between athletes on vegan and non-vegan diets.

In the same vein, a 1986 study conducted on groups of vegan and non-vegan peers showed that there is no difference between their endurance, pulmonary function, limb circumferences and total serum protein. In athletic events that required endurance due to their long duration, the performance of vegans and non-vegans was at par. In 1989, when they consumed the same amount of carbohydrate, there was no difference in the time taken to complete a 10 km race in West Germany. Even though these results show that there is no reduction in performance among vegan athletes, some people still express reservations about vegan diets for athletes.

Calorie and protein requirements

A diet for the vegan athletes should take into account extra energy requirements above that of moderate level activity. The low calorie density in many of the plant foods makes energy requirements become a major consideration.

During exercises, there is an increased protein breakdown and oxidation which is then followed by heightened muscle protein synthesis and further breakdown of proteins during recovery. The rise in the levels of circulating amino acids after one takes a protein-containing meal normally stimulates intramuscular protein synthesis in addition to slightly suppressing muscle breakdown of proteins.

Ingesting just carbohydrates into the body does not induce such increases in protein synthesis by the muscles. Furthermore, protein-containing meals have significant benefits to the immunity, muscle soreness as well as overall health as compared to carbohydrate-only meals.

Because of this, timing of protein content in meals is an important factor in recovery, muscle mass gain and maintenance.

The branched chain amino acids (BCAA) supplements; *isoleucine, valine and leucine* in a ratio of 1:1:2 have been specifically studied for their effects on muscle protein synthesis, performance and recovery. The oxidation of leucine supplements is significantly regulated during endurance exercises thus showing the necessity for increased intake of protein by athletes.

Research has suggested that the BCAA supplements do not affect performance significantly but they attenuate exercise-induced muscle damages and also promote muscle protein synthesis. Plant proteins like *sesame seeds, tofu, pumpkin seeds and sunflower seeds* are great sources of BCAA supplements.

Protein Requirements for Vegan Athletes

Every athlete (both vegan and non vegan) require a greater protein quantity than sedentary individuals. Nevertheless, the amount of protein that is required has been a point of disagreement and confusion between the scientific community and the athletes. Proteins might comprise of 5 percent of the energy that is burned during exercises thus resulting in the need of positive nitrogen balance as raw material for the anabolic processes. This is to replace the losses and build any additional muscle mass. Insufficient ingestion of proteins leads to insufficient recovery and negative nitrogen balance.

Potential Dangers of Excess Proteins

There are no confirmed benefits for any athlete to consume over 200g protein. In fact, excess proteins usually have negative effects on the calcium stores, bone health, cardiovascular health and kidney function.

It is highly encouraged to use whole food protein sources like *tofu, seeds, nuts and hemp seed meals* which have been blended into smoothies and shakes.

It is important to note that isolated proteins powders are micronutrient-poor as compared to whole foods. Furthermore, their usage might pose health risks to individuals since excess animal proteins usually promotes cancers as a result of the increases in insulin growth factor 1-commonly referred to as IGF-1.

Animal proteins are not the only proteins which elevate IGF-1 levels but the isolated proteins from plant different plant sources also have a similar effect. The main factor which defines excess proteins for athletes is yet to be clearly defined due to the scarce studies on protein safety amongst athletes.

Muscle growth

There is a big difference between maximizing health, and maximizing muscle growth and body size. It is clear that a well-designed vegan diet will meet the nutritional demands of an agility and speed athlete like tennis, basketball, skiing, track and soccer. It used to be believed that is was not ideal maximizing muscle growth in larger athletes such as football linebackers or body builders. But there are modern techniques and vegan friendly supplements which can help.

Plant protein concentrates like maca, rice, hemp protein powders and pea are options whenever the athlete wishes to remain vegan or significantly reduce their dependency on the animal products while still supporting a high body mass.

In addition to promoting excellent health, an intelligently and carefully designed supplemented vegan diet will meet the caloric needs and supply enough protein to the body.

Chapter 6: 30 days Meal Plan

Week 1

Day 1
Breakfast: Protein Pancake
Lunch: Buffalo chickpeas and lettuce wraps
Dinner: Sesame Tofu veggies
Day 2
Breakfast: Overnight Chia Oats
Lunch: Lentil and cheese nuggets
Dinner: Red curry mac and cheese
Day 3
Breakfast: Mexican Breakfast
Lunch: Black bean and sweet potato burritos
Dinner: Cauliflower steaks
Day 4
Breakfast: Amaranth quinoa porridge
Lunch: Mac and peas cashew sauce

Dinner: Tempeh burgers
Day 5
Breakfast: Cacao lentil Muffins
Lunch: Chickpeas, mango and curried cauliflower salad
Dinner: Butternut squash tofu jambalaya
Day 6
Breakfast: Goji breakfast bowl
Lunch: vegetable and tofu skewers
Dinner: Vegan high protein chili
Day 7
Breakfast: Hawaiian Toast
Lunch: Baked deep dish pancake
Dinner: Vegan chili for sore muscles

Week 2

Day 8
Breakfast: Breakfast Berry parfait
Lunch: Black bean and veggie soup
Dinner: Tofu and snow pea stir fry with peanut sauce
Day 9
Breakfast: Mini tofu Frittatas
Lunch: Spinach Pasta in peso sauce
Dinner: Crunchy chickpea broccoli and cheese casserole
Day 10
Breakfast: Brownie pancakes
Lunch: Vegan Afredo fettuccine pasta
Dinner: Teriyaki tofu and tempeh casserole
Day 11
Breakfast: Fig and cheese Oatmeal
Lunch: Garlic Pea Shoots
Dinner: Tomato and garlic butter beans
Day 12
Breakfast: Roasted cauliflower salad
Lunch: Tempeh vegetarian chili
Dinner: Cheesy garlicky pull apart pizza bread
Day 13

Breakfast: Mediterranean salad
Lunch: Healthy lentil soup
Dinner: Baked BBQ Tofu with caramelized onions
Day 14
Breakfast: Sweet and smoky BBQ salad
Lunch: lentil vegan soup
Dinner: Vegan Risotto with Sun dried Tomatoes

Week 3

Day 15
Breakfast: Vegetarian Taco Salad
Lunch: Roasted vegetables and lentil soup
Dinner: Quinoa with peas and onion
Day 16
Breakfast: Portobello tofu fajitas
Lunch: Quinoa salad southwestern style
Dinner: Swiss chard with onions and garlic
Day 17
Breakfast: Chocolate-almond butter shake
Lunch: Easy bean burritos
Dinner: Steamed eggplants with peanut dressing
Day 18
Breakfast: Savory tempeh sandwiches
Lunch: Sweet potato, spinach butter bean stew
Dinner: Vegan Greek meatball soup
Day 19
Breakfast: Couscous and chickpea bowls
Lunch: Tofu and mushroom soup
Dinner: Irish lamb stew
Day 20
Breakfast: Berries with Mascarpone on toasted bread
Lunch: Avocado green soup
Dinner: Cauliflower fried rice
Day 21
Breakfast: Chickpea crepes with mushrooms and spinach
Lunch: Spicy black bean soup

Dinner: Red curry mac and cheese

Week 4

Day 22
Breakfast: Vegetarian Taco Salad
Lunch: Red curry quinoa soup
Dinner: Tomato Basil Pasta
Day 23
Breakfast: Savory tempeh sandwiches
Lunch: Split pea soup
Dinner: Red curry mac and cheese
Day 24
Breakfast: Fig and cheese Oatmeal
Lunch: Lunch: Easy bean burritos
Dinner: Irish "lamb" stew
Day 25
Breakfast: Portobello tofu fajitas
Lunch: Burrito and Cauliflower Rice Bowl
Dinner: Vegan Risotto with Sun dried Tomatoes
Day 26
Breakfast: Vegetarian Taco Salad
Lunch: Lentil and cheese nuggets
Dinner: Steamed eggplants with peanut dressing
Day 27
Breakfast: Savory tempeh sandwiches
Lunch: Spicy Snow Pea and Tofu Stir Fry
Dinner: Cauliflower fried rice
Day 28
Breakfast: Fig and cheese Oatmeal
Lunch: Lentil and cheese nuggets
Dinner: Red curry mac and cheese
Day 29
Breakfast: Savory tempeh sandwiches
Lunch: Tofu Sand veggies Buddha bowl
Dinner: Irish "lamb" stew
Day 30

Breakfast: Vegan sheet style pan style tofu
Lunch: Spinach Pasta in peso sauce
Dinner: Steamed eggplants with peanut dressing

Chapter 7: Shopping list

Week 1: Shopping List

-
- 2 packages of vegetable stock
- 11 carrots
- 1 package of cayenne pepper
- 2 packages of cilantro
- 4 lemons
- 2 cans full fat coconut milk
- 3 packages of coconut milk
- 2 packages of psyllium husk
- 1 package of raspberries

2 kiwis
- 3 packages of spinach
- 1 kale
- 24 bananas
- 1 package of spelt flour
- 3 packages of ground flaxseeds
- 1 package of salt
- 2 packages of cinnamon
- 1 package of almonds
- 3 package of hazelnuts
- 2 package of walnuts
- 2 packages of pecans
- 1 package of dried fruit (of choice)
- 2 packages of vanilla extract
- 1 package of couscous
- 1 bottle of maple syrup
- 1 bottle of olive oil
- 3 packages of chickpeas

- 18 onions
- 1 package of cumin
- 1 package of turmeric
- 2 red peppers
- 8 sweet potatoes
- 1 package of ground coriander
- 2 packages of black beans
- 1 package of kidney beans
- 14 tomatoes
- 1 bottle of stevia
- 1 package of black pepper
- 2 packages of mushrooms
- 1 package of chili powder
- 1 package of oregano
- 1 package of thyme
- 1 package of bay leaves
- 1 can of sweet corn
- 1 bottle of lime juice
- 11 red bell peppers
- 1 peach
- 2 mangos
- 1 orange
- 1 pineapple
- 3 packages of blueberries
- 2 coconuts
- 2 packages of rolled oats
- 2 packages of coconut flour
- 2 packages of almond flour
- 1 package of red lentils
- 1 package of coconut flakes (unsweetened)
- 3 packages of hemp seeds
- 1 package of chia seeds
- 2 packages of almond milk
- 1 package of coconut oil
- 1 ginger root
- 1 package of spicy paprika powder
- 5 heads of garlic

- 1 package of tabasco sauce
- 1 bottle of MCT oil
- 1 eggplant
- 1 package of tahini
- 1 bottle of flaxseed oil
- 1 packages of baking powder
- 3 packages of coconut cream
- 1 package of cocoa powder
- 3 packages of tempeh
- 1 purple cabbage
- 2 packages of quinoa
- 1 package of soy sauce
- 1 bottle of sesame oil
- 1 bottle of rice vinegar
- 1 package of chili flakes
- 1 package of red curry paste
- 2 packages of cashews
- 2 packages of nutritional yeast
- 1 package of paprika powder
- 1 bottle of red wine
- 10 potatoes
- 2 fresh parsleys
- 3 celery stalks
- 1 package of miso
- 1 papaya
- 1 yellow bell pepper
- 1 package of frozen greens (i.e. spinach, kale)
- 1 package of mixed frozen berries
- 2 sweet onions
- 1 package of whole wheat flour
- 1 package of smoked paprika powder
- 1 brown bread
- 1 package of green chili flakes
- 1 package of coconut butter
- 1 package of firm tofu
- 2 packages of brown rice
- 1 radish

- 1 cucumber
- 1 package of edamame(shelled)
- 1 package of sesame seeds
- 1 package of cocoa butter
- 1 package of vegan protein powder
- 1 package of dried thyme
- 1 package of broccoli
- 1 package of nutmeg
- 1 package of basil

Week 2: Shopping List

- 3 packages of tempeh
- 3 packages of quinoa
- 7 red bell peppers
- 1 purple cabbage
- 2 sweet potatoes
- 1 kale
- 1 package of broccoli
- 1 bottle of sesame oil
- 1 bottle of soy sauce
- 1 bottle of rice vinegar
- 1 bottle of stevia

16 bananas
- 3 packages of coconut milk
- 2 packages of blueberries
- 2 packages of raspberries
- 2 packages of vanilla extract
- 3 packages of rolled oats
- 1 package of walnuts
- 2 packages of chia seeds
- 3 packages of black beans
- 4 heads of garlic
- 1 sweet onion
- 3 green bell peppers
- 2 packages of whole wheat flour
- 2 packages of smoked paprika powder
- 1 package of cumin

- 1 package of salt
- 1 package of pepper
- 1 brown bread
- 6 tortillas (whole wheat)
- 2 packages of brown rice
- 2 dark vegan chocolates
- 1 package of vanilla flavored vegan protein powder
- 2 kiwis
- 2 packages of spinach
- 2 packages of ground flaxseeds
- 1 pineapple
- 1 mango
- 1 bottle of flaxseed oil
- 1 bottle of olive oil
- 3 packages of hemp seeds
- 2 packages of almond flour
- 3 packages of baking powder
- 7 red onions
- 6 sweet red peppers
- 2 cans (4oz) of green chilis
- 1 package of dry pinto beans
- 1 package of white beans
- 1 package of kidney beans
- 1 roma tomato
- 1 package of paprika powder
- 3 fresh cilantros
- 1 avocado
- 1 package of cilantro
- 1 ginger root
- 3 green onions
- 4 zucchinis
- 1 package of sesame seeds
- 1 jar of peanut butter
- 1 package of chili flakes
- 1 bottle of maple syrup
- 1 package of almonds
- 1 package of pumpkin seeds

- 1 package of dates
- 1 vanilla stick
- 1 bottle of agave nectar
- 3 packages of almond milk
- 1 package of cinnamon
- 1 package of cayenne pepper
- 3 jalapeno peppers
- 1 yellow squash
- 1 bottle of tomato paste
- 2 cans of sweet corn
- 1 package of chili powder
- 1 coconut
- 1 bottle of MCT oil
- 3 packages of cashews
- 1 lime
- 1 package of oat milk
- 1 package of coconut oil
- 1 package of kosher salt
- 1 package of whole wheat spaghetti
- 1 package of tahini
- 2 lemons
- 1 package of Dijon mustard
- 1 package of nutritional yeast
- 1 package of sweet paprika powder
- 1 package of nutmeg
- 1 package of asparagus
- 1 package of peas
- 1 package of baking soda
- 1 package of chickpeas
- 1 package of spicy paprika powder
- 1 package of baby spinach
- 1 package of oregano
- 1 package of avocado oil
- 1 package of garlic powder
- 1 bottle of canola oil

Week 3: Shopping List

- 1 bottle of olive oil
- 3 packages of black beans
- 5 green onions
- 6 red bell peppers
- 1 package of mushrooms
- 1 package of cumin
- 1 package of tabasco sauce
- 1 package of chili powder
- 1 package of salt
- 1 package of sugar
- 2 packages of whole wheat flour
- 1 package of coconut oil
- 1 package of almond butter
- 1 package of almond flour
- 4 packages of almond milk
- 1 bottle of sesame oil
- 2 packages of tofu (1 extra firm)
- 2 packages of baking soda
- 1 package of sesame seeds
- 3 zucchinis

1 package of rolled oats
- 1 package of oat milk
- 1 package of coconut oil
- 3 packages of ground flaxseeds
- 1 package of chia seeds
- 1 package of vanilla sticks
- 1 package of kosher salt
- 1 package of cinnamon
- 1 package of psyllium husk
- 2 cans of full fat coconut milk
- 1 bottle of stevia
- 5 lemons
- 3 packages of raspberries

- 1 package of almonds
- 1 package of coconut flour
- 2 packages of oatmeal

- 13 bananas
- 2 packages of hemp seeds
- 1 package of lentils
- 1 ginger root
- 9 onions (2 yellow onions)
- 1 head of garlic
- 1 package of tomato paste
- 1 package of curry powder
- 1 package of red hot pepper flakes
- 1 jar of diced tomatoes
- 1 package of pepper
- 2 cilantros
- 2 packages of spinach
- 2 kales
- 14 carrots
- 6 celery stalks
- 1 package of nutritional yeast
- 1 package of thyme
- 4 fresh parsleys
- 1 package of vanilla flavored vegan protein powder
- 1 dark vegan chocolate
- 1 bottle of MCT oil
- 1 package of cocoa powder
- 1 package of brown rice
- 1 package of white rice
- 1 package of hazelnut
- 1 package of hazelnut spread
- 1 package of vanilla extract
- 1 can of sweet corn
- 2 packages of quinoa
- 1 tomato
- 6 sweet potatoes
- 1 green bell pepper
- 1 lime
- 2 packages of blueberries
- 1 package of strawberries
- 1 package of blackberries

- 1 bag(300g) of tortilla chips
- 4 large tortillas (whole wheat)
- 2 green apples
- 1 package of sea salt
- 1 package of red pepper flakes
- 1 bottle of cherry vinegar
- 1 package of black pepper
- 1 package of miso
- 1 package of rosemary
- 2 packages of baking powder
- 1 pumpkin
- 1 package of dark chocolate chips (vegan friendly)
- 4 jazz apples
- 4 Red Delicious apples
- 15 oz of tempeh
- 1 purple cabbage
- 1 package of broccoli
- 1 package of soy sauce
- 1 bottle of rice vinegar
- 2 packages of cashews
- 1 package of chili flakes
- 1 package of red curry paste
- 2 packages of coconut milk
- 2 packages of coconut cream
- 1 kiwi
- 2 apples
- 1 pineapple
- 1 mango
- 1 package of couscous
- 1 package of chickpeas
- 1 red pepper
- 1 package of cayenne pepper
- 1 package of cilantro
- 1 package of coriander
- 1 package of ground turmeric
- 2 packages of vegetable stock
- 1 bottle of avocado oil

- 1 package of garlic powder
- 1 package of oregano
- 3 Chioggia beets
- 2 avocados
- 1 package of wasabi powder
- 1 package of sushi rice
- 2 packages of edamame beans
- 1 package of pecans
- 1 package of matcha powder
- 1 package of freeze dried peach powder
- 1 eggplant
- 1 package of tahini
- 1 package of coconut butter
- 1 package of sriracha
- 1 package of brown sugar
- 1 package of wasabi paste
- 1 package of pickled ginger

Week 4: Shopping List

- 2 packages of brown rice
- 1 bottle of olive oil
- 2 packages of portobello mushrooms
- 3 packages of cashews
- 1 package of basil leaves
- 1 bottle of red wine
- 1 package of nutritional yeast
- 1 package of pepper
- 11 onions (3 red, 2 white, 1 green, 2 brown)
- 2 heads of garlic
- 4 carrots
- 7 celery stalks
- 8 sweet potatoes
- 2 kales
- 9 bell peppers (1 green, red and yellow)
- 1 package of thyme
- 1 package of miso
- 4 fresh parsleys

- 1 fresh cilantro
- 1 package of rosemary
- 1 package of miso
- 1 package of peanut butter
- 1 package of cocoa powder
- 3 packages of coconut flour
- 1 package of vanilla flavored vegan protein powder
- 1 package of cumin
- 1 package of cayenne pepper
- 1 package of tahini
- 3 packages of baking powder
- 3 packages of chickpeas
- 4 green apples

13 bananas

- 2 oranges
- 1 ginger root
- 3 lemons
- 2 kiwis
- 3 packages of coconut milk
- 2 packages of walnuts
- 1 package of goji berries
- 1 package of pumpkin seeds
- 2 packages of rolled oats
- 3 packages of almonds
- 1 package of hemp seeds
- 1 package of salt
- 1 bottle of agave nectar
- 1 package of dates
- 2 packages of vanilla extract
- 1 bottle of MCT oil
- 1 bottle of stevia
- 1 package of spinach
- 1 ginger root
- 1 cucumber
- 3 packages of blueberries
- 2 packages of raspberries
- 1 package of coconut butter

- 2 packages of almond flour
- 1 package of almonds
- 1 package of full fat coconut milk
- 1 package of freeze dried blueberry powder
- 2 packages of black beans
- 1 package of white beans
- 2 jalapenos
- 4 large tomatoes
- 1 dark vegan chocolate
- 1 package of hazelnuts
- 2 packages of coconut cream
- 1 bottle of agave nectar
- 1 package of chia seeds
- 1 package of glucomannan powder
- 1 bottle of flaxseed oil
- 1 pumpkin
- 1 package of onion powder
- 1 package of bay leaves
- 1 package of almond butter
- 2 packages of baking soda
- 1 package of paprika powder
- 1 package of coconut oil
- 1 package of tabasco sauce
- 1 eggplant
- 1 pineapple
- 1 mango
- 1 coconut
- 2 cans (14 oz) unsweetened coconut milk
- 1 can diced green chilies
- 1 package of curry powder
- 15 oz tempeh
- 1 purple cabbage
- 2 packages of quinoa
- 1 package of soy sauce
- 1 package of broccoli
- 1 bottle of sesame oil
- 1 bottle of rice vinegar

- 1 package of red curry paste
- 1 package of garlic powder
- 1 package of strawberries
- 1 package of black berries
- 1 zucchini
- 1 bottle of white wine vinegar
- 1 package of vegan BBQ sauce
- 1 lime
- 1 package of cinnamon
- 1 package of whole wheat flour
- 1 package of sesame seeds

Chapter 8: Breakfast Recipes

1. Chocolate-Almond Butter Shake

Preparation time: 3 minutes
Cooking time: 1 minute
Number of servings: 2
Ingredients:
- 2 scoops vegan chocolate protein powder (Real Raw Chocolate Cacao)
- 2 heaping tablespoons maca
- 1 banana, sliced
- Ice cubes, as required
- 2 heaping tablespoons chia seeds
- 2 cups almond milk, unsweetened
- 2 heaping tablespoons creamy, salted almond butter

Directions:
1. Gather all the ingredients and add into a blender.
2. Blend for 30 – 40 seconds or until smooth.
3. Pour into 2 glasses and serve.

Nutrition facts per serving: Calories – 645, Fat – 27 g, Total Carbohydrate – 54 g, Protein – 46 g

2. Savory Tempeh Sandwiches

Preparation time: 5 minutes
Cooking time: 7 minutes
Number of servings: 1
Ingredients:
For sauce mixture:
- 1 ½ tablespoons soy sauce or tamari
- ½ tablespoon apple cider vinegar
- ½ teaspoon smoked paprika
- ¾ tablespoon maple syrup
- 2 small cloves garlic, minced
- Pepper to taste

For sandwich:
- 4 ounces tempeh, cut into 2 – 3 thin slices
- 1 vegan English muffin, split, toasted
- A handful baby spinach
- ½ tablespoon olive oil
- ¼ avocado, peeled, pitted, sliced
- Dijon mustard to taste
- Ketchup

Directions:
1. Add all the ingredients for sauce into a small bowl and stir.
2. Place a skillet over medium heat. Add oil. When the oil is heated, place

tempeh in a single layer and cook until the underside is brown. Flip sides and cook the other side until brown.

3. Add the sauce mixture and stir until well coated. Cook until dry. Flip the tempeh a couple of times while cooking.

4. Spread a little ketchup and Dijon mustard over the cut part of the English muffin.

5. Place tempeh slices on the bottom half of the muffins. Place avocado slices and baby spinach.

6. Cover with the top half of the English muffin and serve.

Nutrition facts per serving: Calories – 573, Fat – 30.3 g, Total Carbohydrate – 54 g, Fiber – 6.4 g, Protein – 29.1 g

3. Protein Pancakes

Preparation time: 5 minutes
Cooking time: 10 minutes
Number of servings: 4
Ingredients:
- 2 cups all-purpose flour

- 2 tablespoons baking powder
- 4 tablespoons pure maple syrup
- ½ cup brown rice protein powder or vegan protein powder
- 1 teaspoon salt
- 2 cups water or more if required

Directions:
1. Add all the dry ingredients into a mixing bowl and stir.
2. Add maple syrup and stir.
3. Add water and stir until just combined. The batter should be thick and of dropping consistency.
4. Place a nonstick pan over medium heat. Spray some cooking spray over it. Pour about ¼ of the batter on the pan. Spread the batter slightly. In a while bubbles will appear on it. Cook until the underside is golden brown. Flip sides and cook the other side.
5. Make the remaining pancakes similarly.

Nutrition facts per serving: Without toppings Calories – 295, Fat – 1.2 g, Total Carbohydrate – 59.9 g, Fiber – 3.5 g, Protein – 15.8 g

4. Couscous and Chickpea Bowls

Preparation time: 5 minutes
Cooking time: 10 minutes
Number of servings: 2
Nutrition facts per serving:
Ingredients:

- 1 medium fennel bulb with fronds, trimmed, cut into ¼ inch wedges, retain the fronds to garnish
- ¼ teaspoon ground coriander
- 5 kalamata olives, halved, pitted
- Juice of ½ orange
- Zest of ½ orange, grated
- Juice of ¼ lemon
- Zest of ¼ lemon
- 1 ½ tablespoons olive oil, divided
- ½ can (from a 15 ounces can) chickpeas, drained, rinsed
- ½ cup instant couscous
- Salt to taste

Directions:

1. Place a skillet over medium heat. Add 1 tablespoon oil. When the oil is heated, add fennel bulb and cook until golden brown. Stir occasionally.
2. Stir in chickpeas, lemon juice, coriander and olives. Stir occasionally and cook for 3-4 minutes. Turn off the heat.
3. Add orange juice into a measuring cup. Pour enough water into the cup to measure up to ¾ cup and pour into a saucepan. Place over medium heat.
4. Add remaining oil, salt, lemon zest and orange zest.
5. When it begins to boil, add couscous and stir. Cover with a lid. Turn off the heat. Let it sit covered for 5 minutes.
6. Fluff with a fork. Divide into 2 bowls.
7. Divide the chickpea mixture and place over the couscous. Sprinkle fennel fronds on top and serve.

Calories – 586, Fat – 16 g, Carbohydrate – 91.2 g, Fiber – 14.9 g, Protein – 22.3 g

5. Berries with Mascarpone on Toasted Bread

Preparation Time: 10 minutes Cooking Time: 0 minute Servings: 1

Ingredients:

1 slice whole-wheat bread
2 tablespoons mascarpone cheese
1/8 cup raspberries
1/8 cup strawberries
1 teaspoon fresh mint leaves

Direction:

Spread the cheese on the bread.
Top with the berries and chopped mint leaves.
Store in food container and refrigerate.
Toast in the oven when ready to eat.

Nutritional Value:

Calories: 326
Total fat: 27.3g
Saturated fat: 14.2g
Cholesterol: 70mg
Sodium: 130mg
Potassium: 115mg
Carbohydrates: 15.1g
Fiber: 4.1g
Sugar: 3g
Protein: 7.9g

6. Overnight Chia Oats

Preparation time: 15minutes + inactive time Cooking time: 20 minutes
Serve: 4
Ingredients:
- 470ml full-fat soy milk
- 90g old-fashioned rolled oats
- 40g chia seeds
- 15ml pure maple syrup
- 25g crushed pistachios

Blackberry Jam:
- 500g blackberries
- 45ml pure maple syrup
- 30ml water
- 45g chia seeds
- 15ml lemon juice

Instructions:
1. Make the oats; in a large bowl, combine soy milk, oats, chia seeds, and maple syrup.
2. Cover and refrigerate overnight.

3. Make the jam; combine blackberries, maple syrup, and water in a saucepan.
4. Simmer over medium heat for 10 minutes.
5. Add the chia seeds and simmer the blackberries for 10 minutes.
6. Remove from heat and stir in lemon juice. Mash the blackberries with a fork and place aside to cool.
7. Assemble; divide the oatmeal among four serving bowls.
8. Top with each bowl blackberry jam.
9. Sprinkle with pistachios before serving.

Nutritional info per serving:
- Calories 362
- Total Fat 13.4g
- Total Carbohydrate 52.6g
- Dietary Fiber 17.4g
- Total Sugars 24.6g
- Protein 12.4g

7. Mexican Breakfast

Preparation time: 10 minutes
Cooking time: 10 minutes
Serve: 4
Ingredients:
- 170g cherry tomatoes, halved
- 1 small red onion, chopped
- 25ml lime juice

- 50ml olive oil
- 1 clove garlic, minced
- 1 teaspoon red chili flakes
- 1 teaspoon ground cumin
- 700g can black beans* (or cooked beans), rinsed
- 4 slices whole-grain bread
- 1 avocado, peeled, pitted
- Salt, to taste

Instructions:
1. Combine tomatoes, onion, lime juice, and 15ml olive oil in a bowl.
2. Season to taste and place aside.
3. Heat 2 tablespoons olive oil in a skillet.
4. Add onion and cook 4 minutes over medium-high heat.
5. Add garlic and cook stirring for 1 minute.
6. Add red chili flakes and cumin. Cook for 30 seconds.
7. Add beans and cook tossing gently for 2 minutes.
8. Stir in ¾ of the tomato mixture and season to taste.
9. Remove from heat.
10. Slice the avocado very thinly.
11. Spread the beans mixture over bread slices. Top with remaining tomato and sliced avocado.
12. Serve.

Nutritional info per serving:
- Calories 476
- Total Fat 21.9g
- Total Carbohydrate 52.4g
- Dietary Fiber 19.5g
- Total Sugars 5.3g
- Protein 17.1g

8. Amaranth Quinoa porridge

Preparation time: 5 minutes
Cooking time: 35 minu

Serve: 2

Ingredients:
- 85g quinoa
- 70g amaranth
- 460ml water
- 115ml unsweetened soy milk
- ½ teaspoon vanilla paste
- 15g almond butter
- 30ml pure maple syrup
- 10g raw pumpkin seeds
- 10g pomegranate seeds

Instructions:
1. Combine quinoa, amaranth, and water.
2. Bring to a boil over medium-high heat.
3. Reduce heat and simmer the grains, stirring occasionally, for 20 minutes.
4. Stir in milk and maple syrup.
5. Simmer for 6-7 minutes. Remove from the heat and stir in vanilla, and almond butter.
6. Allow the mixture to stand for 5 minutes.
7. Divide the porridge between two bowls.
8. Top with pumpkin seeds and pomegranate seeds.

9. Serve.

Nutritional info per serving:
- Calories 474
- Total Fat 13.3g
- Total Carbohydrate 73.2g
- Dietary Fiber 8.9g
- Total Sugars 10g
- Protein 17.8g

9. Cacao Lentil Muffins

Preparation time: 10 minutes
Cooking time: 15 minutes
Serve: 12 muffins (2 per serving) Ingredients:
- 195g cooked red lentils
- 50ml melted coconut oil
- 45ml pure maple syrup
- 60ml unsweetened almond milk
- 60ml water
- 60g raw cocoa powder
- 120g whole-wheat flour
- 20g peanut flour
- 10g baking powder, aluminum-free
- 70g Vegan chocolate chips

Instructions:
1. Preheat oven to 200C/400F.
2. Line 12-hole muffin tin with paper cases.
3. Place the cooked red lentils in a food blender. Blend on high until smooth.
4. Transfer the lentils puree into a large bowl.
5. Stir in coconut oil, maple syrup, almond milk, and water.
6. In a separate bowl, whisk cocoa powder, whole-wheat flour, peanut flour, and baking powder.
7. Fold in liquid ingredients and stir until just combined.
8. Add chocolate chips and stir until incorporated.
9. Divide the batter among 12 paper cases.
10. Tap the muffin tin gently onto the kitchen counter to remove air.
11. Bake the muffins for 15 minutes.
12. Cool muffins on a wire rack.
13. Serve.

Nutritional info per serving:
- Calories 372
- Total Fat 13.5g
- Total Carbohydrate 52.7g
- Dietary Fiber 12.9g
- Total Sugars 13g
- Protein 13.7g

10. Chickpea Crepes with Mushrooms and Spinach

Preparation time: 20 minutes + inactive time Cooking time: 15 minutes

Serve: 4

Ingredients:

Crepes:
- 140g chickpea flour
- 30g peanut flour
- 5g nutritional yeast
- 5g curry powder
- 350ml water
- Salt, to taste

Filling:
- 10ml olive oil - 4 portabella mushroom caps, thinly sliced - 1 onion, thinly sliced - 30g baby spinach - Salt, and pepper, to taste Vegan mayo:
- 60ml aquafaba
- 1/8 teaspoon cream of tartar
- ¼ teaspoon dry mustard powder
- 15ml lemon juice
- 5ml raw cider vinegar

- 15ml maple syrup
- 170ml avocado oil
- Salt, to taste

Instructions:
1. Make the mayo; combine aquafaba, cream of tartar, mustard powder. Lemon juice, cider vinegar, and maple syrup in a bowl.
2. Beat with a hand mixer for 30 seconds.
3. Set the mixer to the highest speed. Drizzle in avocado oil and beat for 10 minutes or until you have a mixture that resembles mayonnaise.
4. Of you want paler (in the color mayo) add more lemon juice.
5. Season with salt and refrigerate for 1 hour.
6. Make the crepes; combine chickpea flour, peanut flour, nutritional yeast, curry powder, water, and salt to taste in a food blender.
7. Blend until smooth.
8. Heat large non-stick skillet over medium-high heat. Spray the skillet with some cooking oil.
9. Pour ¼ cup of the batter into skillet and with a swirl motion distribute batter all over the skillet bottom.
10. Cook the crepe for 1 minute per side. Slide the crepe onto a plate and keep warm.
11. Make the filling; heat olive oil in a skillet over medium-high heat.
12. Add mushrooms and onion and cook for 6-8 minutes.
13. Add spinach and toss until wilted, for 1 minute.
14. Season with salt and pepper and transfer into a large bowl.
15. Fold in prepared vegan mayo.
16. Spread the prepared mixture over chickpea crepes. Fold gently and serve.

Nutritional info per serving:
- Calories 428
- Total Fat 13.3g
- Total Carbohydrate 60.3g
- Dietary Fiber 18.5g
- Total Sugars 13.2g
- Protein 22.6g

11. Goji Breakfast Bowl

Preparation time: 10 minutes
Serve: 2
Ingredients:
- 15g chia seeds
- 10g buckwheat
- 15g hemp seeds
- 20g Goji berries
- 235mml vanilla soy milk

Instructions:
1. Combine chia, buckwheat, hemp seeds, and Goji berries in a bowl.
2. Heat soy milk in a saucepan until start to simmer.
3. Pour the milk over "cereals".
4. Allow the cereals to stand for 5 minutes.
5. Serve.

Nutritional info per serving:
- Calories 339
- Total Fat 14.3g
- Total Carbohydrate 41.8g
- Dietary Fiber 10.5g
- Total Sugars 20g
- Protein 13.1g

12. Breakfast Berry Parfait

Preparation time: 10 minutes
Serve: 1
Ingredients:
- 250g soy yogurt
- 10g wheat germ
- 40g raspberries
- 40g blackberries
- 30ml maple syrup
- 10g slivered almonds

Instructions:
1. Pour 1/3 of soy yogurt in a parfait glass.
2. Top with raspberries and 1 tablespoon wheat germ.
3. Repeat layer with blackberries and remaining wheat germ.
4. Finish with soy yogurt.
5. Drizzle the parfait with maple syrup and sprinkle with almonds.
6. Serve.

Nutritional info per serving:
- Calories 327
- Total Fat 9.4g

- Total Carbohydrate 48.7g
- Dietary Fiber 8.4g
- Total Sugars 29.3g
- Protein 15.6g

13. Mini Tofu Frittatas

Preparation time: 15 minutes
Cooking time: 25 minutes
Serve: 12 mini frittatas (3 per serving) Ingredients:
- 450g firm tofu, drained
- 115ml soy milk
- 5g mild curry powder
- 15ml olive oil
- 20g chopped scallions
- 80g corn kernels, fresh
- 140g cherry tomatoes, quartered
- 75g baby spinach
- Salt and pepper, to taste

Pesto for serving:
- 15g fresh basil
- 10g walnuts
- 1 clove garlic, peeled
- 10g lemon juice
- 5g nutritional yeast
- 20ml olive oil

- 30ml water
- Salt, to taste

Instructions:
1. Make the frittatas; Preheat oven to 180C/350F.
2. Line 12-hole mini muffin pan with paper cases.
3. Combine tofu, soy milk, and curry powder in a food blender. Blend until smooth.
4. Heat olive oil in a skillet.
5. Add scallions and cook 3 minutes.
6. Add corn and tomatoes. Cook 2 minutes.
7. Add spinach, and cook stirring for 1 minute. Season to taste.
8. Stir the veggies into tofu mixture.
9. Divide the tofu-vegetable mixture among 12 paper cases.
10. Bake the frittata for 25 minutes.
11. In the meantime, make the pesto; combine basil, walnuts, lemon juice, and nutritional yeast in a food processor.
12. Process until smooth.
13. Add olive oil and process until smooth.
14. Scrape down the sides and add water. Process until creamy.
15. To serve; remove frittatas from the oven. Cool on a wire rack.
16. Remove the frittatas from the muffin tin. Top each with pesto.
17. Serve.

Nutritional info per serving:
- Calories 220
- Total Fat 14.2g
- Total Carbohydrate 13.5g
- Dietary Fiber 4.5g
- Total Sugars 4g
- Protein 15g

14. Brownie Pancakes

Preparation time: 10 minutes
Cooking time: 5 minutes
Serve: 2
Ingredients:
- 35g cooked black beans
- 30g all-purpose flour
- 25g peanut flour
- 25g raw cocoa powder
- 5g baking powder, aluminum free
- 15ml pure maple sugar
- 60g unsweetened soy milk
- 35g organic applesauce
- ½ teaspoon vanilla paste
- 10g crushed almonds

Instructions:
1. Combine cooked black beans, all-purpose flour, peanut flour, cocoa powder, and baking powder in a bowl.
2. In a separate bowl, whisk maple syrup, soy milk, applesauce, and vanilla.
3. Fold liquid ingredients into dry and whisk until smooth. You can also toss ingredients into a food blender and blend.
4. Heat large non-stick skillet over medium-high heat. Spray the skillet with some cooking oil.
5. Pour ¼ cup of batter into skillet. Sprinkle with some almonds.

6. Cook the pancakes on each side for 1 ½ - 2 minutes.
7. Serve warm, drizzled with desired syrup.

Nutritional info per serving:
- Calories 339
- Total Fat 9.5g
- Total Carbohydrate 46.8g
- Dietary Fiber 11.2g
- Total Sugars 6.5g
- Protein 26.5g

15. Fig & Cheese Oatmeal

Preparation Time: 10 minutes Cooking Time: 0 minute Servings: 1

Ingredients:

- ½ cup water
- ½ cup rolled oats
- Pinch salt
- 2 tablespoons dried figs, sliced
- 2 tablespoons ricotta cheese
- 2 teaspoons honey
- 1 tablespoon almonds, toasted and sliced

Direction:

1. Put the water, oats and salt in a glass jar with lid.

2. Shake to blend well.
3. Refrigerate for up to 5 days.
4. Top with the remaining ingredients when ready to serve.

Nutritional Value:
Calories: 294
Total fat: 8.5g
Saturated fat: 2.3g
Cholesterol: 10mg
Sodium: 182mg
Potassium: 362mg
Carbohydrates: 47.5g
Fiber: 6.6g
Sugar: 16g
Protein: 10.4g

Pumpkin Oats

Preparation Time: 10 minutes Cooking Time: 0 minute Servings: 1
Ingredients:

- ½ cup rolled oats
- ½ cup almond milk
- ¼ cup ricotta cheese
- 2 tablespoons pumpkin puree
- 1 tablespoon maple syrup
- ¼ teaspoon vanilla
- 1/8 teaspoon ground nutmeg

Direction:

1. Combine all the ingredients in a glass jar with lid.
2. Refrigerate for up to 5 days.

Nutritional Value:
Calories: 344
Total fat: 10g
Saturated fat: 3.8g
Cholesterol: 19mg
Sodium: 179mg
Potassium: 364mg

Carbohydrates: 51.7g
Fiber: 5.7g
Sugar: 16g

15. Roasted Cauliflower Salad

Preparation time: 15 minutes
Cooking time: 45 minutes
Number of servings: 10
Nutritional facts per serving:
Ingredients:
For vinaigrette:
- ½ cup olive oil
- 4 tablespoons honey
- 4 teaspoons finely grated ginger
- ½ cup white wine vinegar
- 1 teaspoon Dijon mustard

For salad:
- 1 1/3 cups pearl barley, rinsed a couple of times

- 2 tablespoons olive oil
- ½ cup finely chopped red onion
- Salt to taste
- Pepper to taste
- 2 heads cauliflower, cut into bite size florets (about 20 cups)
- 1 cup cashews
- 2 cans (14.5 ounces each) chickpeas, drained, rinsed

Directions:
1. Follow the directions on the package and cook the barley.
2. Place cauliflower in a large bowl. Drizzle oil over it. Toss well. Season with salt and pepper and toss well.
3. Transfer onto a large baking sheet. Spread it evenly.
4. Bake in a preheated oven at 400° F for about 35-45 minutes or until golden brown at few spots. Stir once half way through baking.
5. Place cashews on the baking sheet and bake for 4-5 minutes or until light brown.
6. To make vinaigrette: Add all the ingredients for vinaigrette into a small jar. Fasten the lid and shake the jar vigorously until well combined.
7. Add cauliflower into a bowl. Add rest of the ingredients for salad and toss well.
8. Pour dressing on top. Toss well.

Calories –442, Fat – 21 g, Carbohydrate – 77 g, Fiber – 21 g, Protein – 23 g

16. Mediterranean Salad

Preparation time: 10 minutes

Cooking time: 10 minutes
Number of servings: 2
Nutrition facts per serving:
Ingredients:
For salad:
- ½ cup dry couscous
- ½ cup roasted red peppers
- ½ cup marinated artichokes
- 1 cup baby spinach
- 5 ounces roasted pine nut hummus
- ½ cup diced cucumbers
- ½ package (from an 8 ounces package) store bought falafels

For lemon vinaigrette:
- 1 tablespoon olive oil
- ½ teaspoon dried oregano
- 1 tablespoon lemon juice
- Salt to taste

Directions:

1. Add all the ingredients for dressing into a small jar. Fasten the lid and shake the jar vigorously until well combined. Refrigerate until use. It can last for 5 days.
2. Cook the couscous following the directions on the package. Fluff with a fork and let it cool.
3. Add all the ingredients for salad into a bowl (including couscous) and toss well.
4. Pour dressing over the salad. Toss well and serve.

Calories –450, Fat – 25 g, Carbohydrate – 46 g, Fiber – 5 g, Protein – 19 g

17. Sweet and Smoky BBQ Salad

Preparation time: 10 minutes
Cooking time: 20 minutes
Number of servings: 2
Nutrition facts per serving:
Ingredients:
- ¾ cup quinoa
- ½ can (from a 15 ounces can) black beans, drained, rinsed
- 1 small onions, chopped
- 1 cup arugula
- ½ container (from a 10 ounces container) Sabra Sweet and Smoky BBQ hummus with Jackfruit and Smoked Paprika
- ¼ pound cherry tomatoes, halved

- ½ mango, peeled, deseeded, cubed

For chili lime vinaigrette:
- 1 tablespoon lime juice
- 1 tablespoon olive oil
- ½ teaspoon chili powder
- ½ teaspoon Dijon mustard
- ¼ teaspoon salt or to taste

Directions:
1. Add all the ingredients for dressing into a small jar. Fasten the lid and shake the jar vigorously until well combined. Refrigerate until use. It can last for 5 days.
2. Cook the quinoa following the directions on the package. Fluff with a fork and let it cool.
3. Add all the ingredients for salad into a bowl (including quinoa) and toss well.
4. Pour dressing over the salad. Toss well and serve.

Calories –450, Fat – 25 g, Carbohydrate – 46 g, Fiber – 5 g, Protein – 19 g

18. Vegetarian Taco Salad

Preparation time: 10 minutes
Cooking time: 2 minutes
Number of servings: 4
Nutrition facts per serving:
Ingredients:
For dressing:
- 4 tablespoons tahini

- 1 teaspoon maple syrup or agave nectar
- 4 tablespoons olive oil
- 4 teaspoons chili powder
- Juice of 2 limes

For the salad:
- 2 cups chopped cherry tomatoes
- 1 cup cooked corn, fresh or frozen
- 8 cups Romaine lettuce or any other greens of your choice
- 2 cups cooked or canned black beans
- 1 avocado, peeled, pitted, diced

Directions:

1. Add all the ingredients for dressing into a small jar. Fasten the lid and shake the jar vigorously until well combined. Add water to dilute if desired. Refrigerate until use.
2. Add all the ingredients for salad into a bowl and toss well. Drizzle the dressing on top. Toss well and serve.

Calories –703, Fat – 31 g, Carbohydrate – 87 g, Fiber – 25 g, Protein – 28 g

19. Roasted Chickpea Gyros

Preparation time: minutes
Cooking time: minutes
Number of servings: 2
Nutrition facts per serving:
Ingredients:
- ½ can (from a 15 ounces can) chickpeas, drained, rinsed
- ½ tablespoon paprika
- 1/8 teaspoon cayenne pepper or to taste
- ¼ tablespoon pepper or to taste
- Salt to taste
- ½ tablespoon olive oil
- 2 pita flatbreads
- 1 small onion, thinly sliced
- ½ tomato, thinly sliced
- ½ cup vegan tzatziki
- 1 large lettuce leaf, chopped

Directions:
1. Grease a baking sheet with some cooking spray.

2. Dry the chickpeas by patting with paper towels.
3. Place chickpeas in a bowl. Sprinkle salt and spices over it and toss well.
4. Transfer onto the prepared baking sheet.
5. Bake in a preheated oven at 400° F for about 20 minutes until light brown. Remove from the oven.
6. Smear tzatziki on one half of the pita. Divide the chickpeas and vegetables and place over the tzatziki. Fold the other half over the filling and serve.

Calories – 331, Fat – 12.6 g, Total Carbohydrate – 45 g, Fiber – 7.5 g, Protein – 11.5 g

20. Portobello Tofu Fajitas

Preparation time: 10 minutes
Cooking time: 12 – 13 minutes
Number of servings: 2
Ingredients:
- 2 large Portobello mushrooms, cut into thick slices
- 1 ½ red bell peppers, thinly sliced

- ½ pound extra-firm tofu, chopped
- 1 onion, thinly sliced
- 1 tablespoon lime juice
- ½ tablespoon coconut oil
- ½ tablespoon taco seasoning
- ¼ cup chopped cilantro

Directions:

1. Place a skillet over medium heat. Add oil. When the oil is heated, add onion and bell pepper and sauté until slightly tender.
2. Add tofu and cook for a couple of minutes. Stir in the mushrooms and taco seasoning. Cook until vegetables are soft.
3. Add lime juice and salt and mix well. Remove from heat.
4. Serve over tortillas with toppings of your choice.

Nutrition facts per serving: Without tortillas or toppings Calories – 335, Fat – 15 g, Total Carbohydrate – 31 g, Protein – 18.5 g

Chapter 9: Lunch Recipes

21. Tofu and Veggies Buddha Bowl

Serving Size: 1
Servings per Recipe: 6
Calories: 957 calories per serving
Preparation Time: 10 minutes
Cooking Time: 40 minutes
Ingredients
- Sesame oil - 2 tablespoons
- Sweet mirin - 2 tablespoons
- Fiery Spice Blend - 1 tablespoon
- Kosher salt - 1 teaspoon
- Extra-firm tofu - 16 ounces
- Sweet potatoes (rinse and peel) – 2 medium
- Broccoli crowns - 2 medium
- Quinoa (cooked) - 1 kg
- Purple cabbage (thinly sliced) - 3 cups
- English cucumber (julienned) - 3 cups
- Avocado (thinly sliced) - 1 large
- Peanuts (roasted) - ⅓ cup

- Garnish
- Fresh cilantro leaves – 1 tablespoon
- Fresh mint leaf (torn) - 3 tablespoons
- Fiery peanut sauce
- Sesame oil - 2 tablespoons
- Apple cider vinegar - 2 tablespoons
- Fiery Spice Blend - 1 tablespoon
- Cold water - ⅓ cup
- Kosher salt – as per taste

Directions

1. Start by preheating the oven by setting the temperature to 400 degrees Fahrenheit.
2. Now let us prepare the marinade for tofu. Take a medium-sized mixing bowl and add in the mirin, sesame oil, salt and fiery spice blend. Mix well.
3. Toss in the tofu cubes and mix well. Ensure all cubes are well coated. Cover it using a plastic wrap and place it in the refrigerator for about an hour.
4. Now take a large pot and fill it with cold water. Add salt and mix well. Toss in the sweet potatoes. Let it boil on medium-high flame.
5. Reduce the flame and let the sweet potatoes boil for 20 minutes.
6. Once done, remove the sweet potatoes from the water and set aside. In the same water, blanch the broccoli florets for about a minute and a half.
7. Remove the broccoli and add transfer them to ice water. Let them sit in an ice bath for a minute. Remove and set aside on a plate lined with a paper towel. This will help in removing excess liquid.
8. Cut the boiled sweet potatoes lengthwise through the center. Further, cut into half-moon measuring 1 ½ -inch. Sprinkle with salt.
9. Take a baking sheet and grease it lightly. Place the sweet potato and marinated tofu onto the sheet.
10. Place it in the preheated oven and bake for about 20 minutes.
11. While the tofu and sweet potatoes are cooking. Let us prepare the fiery peanut sauce.
12. Take a medium mixing bowl and add in the apple cider vinegar, peanut butter, ¼ water and spice blend. Whisk well to combine.
13. Now, let us assemble the 6 tofu and veggies Buddha bowls. For this, in a bowl add 1 cup of quinoa, then follow it with 2 ½ ounces of tofu, ½ a cup of sweet potato, ½ a cup of broccoli, ½ a cup of purple cabbage, ½ a cup of

cucumber and few slices of avocado.
14. Drizzle 2 tablespoons of peanut sauce and further top it with cilantro, mint and crushed peanuts.

Nutrition Information
Fat – 28 g
Carbohydrates – 144 g
Protein – 39 g

22. Vegan Sheet Pan 3 Style Tofu

Serving Size: 1
Servings per Recipe: 4
Calories: 350 calories per serving
Preparation Time: 5 minutes
Cooking Time: 40 minutes (2-3 hours additional)

Ingredients
- Extra firm tofu – 28 ounces
- Vegan barbeque sauce – as per taste
- Vegan teriyaki sauce – as per taste
- Tofu cutlets
- Soy sauce (low sodium) - 2 tablespoons
- Garlic powder (divided) - ¾ teaspoon
- All-purpose flour - ½ cup
- Corn starch - 1 tablespoon
- Non-dairy milk (unsweetened) - ½ cup

- Panko bread crumbs - ½ cup
- Nutritional yeast - 1 tablespoon
- Paprika - 1 teaspoon
- Cayenne pepper - ¼ teaspoon
- Kosher salt - ½ teaspoon
- Pepper - ¼ teaspoon
- Olive oil – as required

Directions

1. Start by preheating the oven by setting the temperature to 400 degrees Fahrenheit.
2. Take 2 tofu blacks and slice them through the center. Place all the blocks on the kitchen towel and cover with another. Place a baking tray and a heavy object to drain excess liquid. Let it sit for about an hour.
3. Take 2 tofu blocks and place them on a baking dish. Drizzle low-sodium soy sauce over each side evenly. Sprinkle gently with ¼ teaspoon of garlic powder on each side. Coat evenly. Let the tofu marinate for about 10 minutes.
4. Take a small mixing bowl and add in the cornstarch and flour. Mix well to combine. Take another bowl and pour in the milk.
5. Take a third mixing bowl and toss in the nutritional yeast, bread crumbs, paprika, cayenne pepper, remaining garlic powder, pepper and salt. Mix well to combine.
6. Take the marinated tofu and coat it with cornstarch mixture and then dip it milk. Again coat it in cornstarch mixture, dip in milk and finish by coating it with bread crumb and spice mixture.
7. Repeat the procedure with the second tofu block.
8. Take a baking dish and lightly grease it with olive oil. Place the tofu blocks and brush them using olive oil on each side.
9. Take the non-breaded tofu pieces and place them on the baking dish.
10. Take the teriyaki sauce and brush it on both sides of one non-breaded tofu piece.
11. Take the barbeque sauce and brush it on both sides of one non-breaded tofu piece.
12. Place the baking dish in the preheated oven and cook for about 15 minutes. Flip all the four pieces and cook for another 15 minutes.
13. Remove the baking dish from the oven and transfer the tofu cutlets onto

a wooden chopping board. Cut into cubes.
14. Serve them with salads or use them in sandwiches or wraps.
Note – These baked tofu cutlets can be stored in the refrigerator for up to 5 days.

Nutrition Information
Fat – 17 g
Carbohydrates – 28 g
Protein – 24 g

23. Buffalo Chickpeas and Lettuce Wraps

Serving Size: 1
Servings per Recipe: 2
Calories: 625 calories per serving
Preparation Time: 10 minutes
Cooking Time: 5 minutes
Ingredients
- Olive oil - 1 tablespoon
- Chickpeas - 1 can (15 ounces)
- Garlic powder - ½ teaspoon
- Salt - 1 pinch
- Buffalo sauce - ¼ cup
- Hummus - ⅓ cup

- Lemon juice - 1 tablespoon
- Water - 1 tablespoon
- Tortillas - 2 large
- Romaine lettuce – 4 leaves
- Red onion (sliced)
- Tomato (sliced)

Directions

1. Take a large nonstick saucepan and pour 1 tablespoon of olive oil. Place it over medium flame.
2. Once the oil starts simmering, toss in the chickpeas and cook for about 3 minutes.
3. Add in the salt, buffalo sauce and garlic powder. Cook for about 2 minutes. The sauce should be thick and coat the chickpeas well. Keep aside.
4. Take a small mixing bowl and add in the hummus, water and lemon juice. Whisk well to combine.
5. Now take the tortillas and place 2 romaine lettuce leaves in the center. Top it with chickpeas, sliced tomatoes and sliced red onions.
6. Pour the hummus dressing on top.
7. Fold the edges and roll it in the shape of a burrito. Cut in equal halves.
8. Repeat the process with the other tortilla.

Nutrition Information

Fat – 19 g

Carbohydrates – 89 g

Protein – 25 g

24. Lentil and Cheese Nuggets

Serving Size: 1
Servings per Recipe: 6
Calories: 217 calories per serving
Preparation Time: 10 minutes (3 hours additional)
Cooking Time: 20 minutes
Ingredients
- Lentils - 1 ½ cups
- Carrot (sliced) - 1
- Corn - ½ cup
- Pea - ½ cup
- Vegan cheddar cheese (shredded) - 1 cup
- Dried oregano - 1 teaspoon
- Salt - 1 teaspoon
- Pepper - 1 teaspoon
- Red pepper flakes - ½ teaspoon
- Garlic - 1 clove

Directions
1. Start by soaking the lentil for 3 hours in cold water.
2. Once the lentils are done soaking, set the temperature of the oven at 400 degrees Fahrenheit and let it preheat.
3. Take a baking tray and line it using parchment paper.
4. Now take a food processor and add in the carrots, peas, corns, vegan cheddar cheese, salt, oregano, pepper, garlic, soaked lentils and red pepper flakes. Pulse to mix all the ingredients well.

5. Form nuggets by taking 1 tablespoon of lentil mixture using your hands. Repeat the process with the rest of the mixture.
6. Place all the nuggets onto the lined baking tray. Bake for about 10 minutes. Flip over and bake for another 10 minutes.
7. Remove the baking tray from the oven and let the cutlets rest for about 5 minutes. Serve!

Nutrition Information
Fat – 7 g
Carbohydrates – 24 g
Protein – 13 g

25. Black Bean and Sweet Potato Burritos

Serving Size: 1
Servings per Recipe: 3
Calories: 542 calories per serving
Preparation Time: 10 minutes
Cooking Time: 30 minutes
Ingredients
- Sweet potatoes (peel and cut in cubes) - 2 medium Olive oil – as per taste
- Smoked paprika - ½ teaspoon
- Garlic powder - ½ teaspoon

- Kosher salt – as per taste
- Pepper – as per taste
- Yellow onion (diced) - ½ medium
- Jalapeño (diced) - ½ medium
- Garlic (minced) - 1 clove
- Chili powder - 1 teaspoon
- Ground cumin - ½ teaspoon
- Cayenne pepper – as per taste
- Black beans (drain and rinse) - 1 can (15 ounces) Corn - ¾ cup
- Flour tortillas - 3 large
- Lettuce leaves (chopped) – for serving
- Tomato (diced) – for serving
- Vegan cheddar cheese (shredded) - for serving Guacamole - for serving

Directions

1. Start by preheating the oven by setting the temperature to 400 degrees Fahrenheit.
2. Take a nonstick baking tray and toss in the cubed sweet potatoes. Drizzle olive oil on top. Also sprinkle the garlic powder, paprika, pepper and salt. Toss well to ensure the sweet potatoes are evenly coated.
3. Place the tray in the preheated oven and bake for about 10 minutes. Flip over the sweet potatoes and bake for another 10 minutes.
4. Take a nonstick saucepan and drizzle olive oil. Place it over medium flame.
5. Once the oil starts simmering, toss in the onions and cook for about 4 minutes.
6. Add in the garlic, jalapeno, cumin, cayenne pepper and chili powder. Cook for another 3 minutes.
7. Toss in the black beans, pepper and salt and cook for 3 minutes. The ingredients should completely heat through.
8. Let us now assemble the burrito, place one of the tortillas on a flat surface. Add 1/3 of corn and bean mixture, 1/3 of prepared sweet potatoes, little bit of lettuce, guacamole, diced tomatoes and vegan cheddar cheese in the center. Fold in the edges and roll to form a burrito. Repeat the process the remaining tortillas.

9. Cut each burrito in two equal halves and serve.

Nutrition Information
Fat – 12 g
Carbohydrates – 95 g
Protein – 16 g

26. Mac and Peas and Cashew Sauce

Serving Size: 1
Servings per Recipe: 4
Calories: 567 calories per serving
Preparation Time: 10 minutes
Cooking Time: 10 minutes
Ingredients

- Yellow potatoes (peel and cut in cubes) - 2
- Carrot (peel and cut in 1-inch pieces) - 1 medium Onion (peel and cut in 4 quarters) - 1
- Cashews - ½ cup
- Salt - 1 teaspoon
- Garlic powder - 1 teaspoon
- Onion powder - 1 teaspoon
- Nutritional yeast - 2 tablespoons
- Macaroni (cooked) - 16 ounces

- Green peas - 2 cups
- Paprika – as per taste

Directions

1. Start by taking a large pot with water and place it over high heat. When it comes to a boil add in the carrots, onions and potatoes. Cover the pot with a lid and boil for about 10 minutes.
2. Remove the boiled vegetables using a strainer. Reserve about 2 cups of water for later use.
3. Take a blender and add in the boiled carrots, onions, potatoes, cashews, salt, garlic powder, onion powder, nutritional yeast, paprika along with the reserved water. Blend well to form smooth puree like consistency.
4. Place the cooked macroni in a large mixing bowl and pour the prepared puree on top. Toss in the green peas and mix well. Serve!

Nutrition Information

Fat – 7 g

Carbohydrates – 105 g

Protein – 21 g

27. Chickpea, Mango and Curried Cauliflower Salad

Prep Time: 10 minutes
Cook Time: 25 minutes
Total Time: 35 minutes
Servings: 4

Ingredients
- 1 teaspoon curry powder
- 1 teaspoon sugar
- 1 teaspoon ground mustard
- 1 teaspoon ground coriander
- ½ teaspoon ground turmeric
- ½ teaspoon ground cumin
- 3 tablespoons olive oil more as needed
- 1 medium yellow onion thinly sliced
- 1 cup canned chickpeas drained, rinsed and warmed through slightly
- 1 head of cauliflower cut into 1-inch florets, blanch for 2 minutes in boiling water and then pat dry
- 2 large mangoes peeled, pitted and chopped into ½-inch pieces

- 1 jalapeno stemmed, seeded and diced small
- 1 cup chopped cilantro
- 2 tablespoons lime juice
- 2 cups baby spinach
- 1 cup baby arugula
- Salt and black pepper

Direction

- Blend the curry powder, cinnamon, ground mustard, coriander, cumin, ½ teaspoon of kosher salt, and ¼ teaspoon black pepper in a small bowl. Set it aside.
- Put the olive oil in a large skillet. Add the onion and cook at high heat for about 6 minutes. Attach the mixture of spices and turn the heat to medium-low. Cook an extra 6 minutes. Move to a wide bowl and add to the same bowl the chickpeas. Keep the pan at medium heat.
- Add the cauliflower to the same pan where the onion was cooked. If required, add more olive oil. Cook in the remaining spice mixture for about 5 minutes or until the cauliflower is seasoned and cooked clean. Use the onion and chickpeas to transfer the cauliflower to the bowl. Let sit for approximately 20 minutes at room temperature.
- Apply the pineapple, jalapeno, coriander, lime juice, spinach, and arugula to the dish. Toss in order to disperse the ingredients evenly. Adjust seasoning to taste and serve as soon as possible.
- Enjoy!

Nutrition Information

Fat – 10 g

Carbohydrates – 13 g

Protein – 19 g

28. Vegetable and Tofu Skewers

Serving Size: 1
Servings per Recipe: 4
Calories: 187 calories per serving
Preparation Time: 10 minutes (1 hour additional)
Cooking Time: 17 minutes
Ingredients
- Water - ½ cup
- Maple syrup - ¼ cup
- Soy sauce - 3 tablespoons
- BBQ sauce - 2 tablespoons
- Oil - 1 tablespoon
- Garlic powder - 1 tablespoon
- Sriracha - 1 tablespoon
- Black pepper - 1 teaspoon
- Firm tofu - 15 ounces
- Peppers - 2
- Onions – 2 medium
- Zucchini - 1
- Skewers - 4

Directions
1. Start by taking a shallow dish and fill it with water. Soak the wooden

skewers in the same as this will prevent them from burning.
2. Take the zucchini and slice it in round slices. Also cut peppers and onions in squares.
3. In the meanwhile, take a quarter plate and line it with a paper towel. Place tofu and cover it with another paper towel and place a plate on top.
4. Place the tofu along with plates in the microwave for about 3 minutes.
5. Remove the tofu and place it on a chopping board. Cut it into cubes.
6. Take a glass measuring cup and add in the water, soy sauce, maple syrup, oil, barbeque sauce, pepper, Sriracha and garlic powder. Stir well.
7. Take a rectangle storage box and place the tofu inside it. Pour the prepared sauce over tofu and cover it with a lid. Place it in the refrigerator for about an hour.
8. Once done, remove the tofu from marinade. Keep aside
9. Take a nonstick saucepan and pour the marinating liquid to the saucepan. Place it over low flame for about 10 minutes. Put off the flame once the sauce starts to thicken.
10. Remove the skewers from the water and start assembling them.
11. Take 1 skewer and start assembling by alternating between zucchini, onion, pepper and tofu.
12. Take a grill pan and place in medium flame. Cook each assembled skewer on each side for about 4 minutes. Glaze each side with sauce while cooking.
13. All sides should have a light char as this will add nice smoky flavor to the dish.

Nutrition Information
Fat – 9 g
Carbohydrates – 17 g
Protein – 11 g

29. Baked deep-dish apple pancake

Makes: one 8-to 9-inch (20 to 23 cm) pancake;
Serves 6 to 8
TIME: 10 minutes to prep, 30 to 35 minutes to bake

Ingredients
- 4 tart apples (such as Gala, Honeycrisp, or Granny Smith), peeled, cored, and thinly sliced
- ¼ cup (30 g) chopped walnuts or pecans, optional
- 1 teaspoon ground cinnamon
- 1½ cups (225 g) whole wheat flour
- 2 teaspoons baking powder
- ¼ teaspoon plus 1/8 teaspoon salt
- 1 cup (240 ml) light or full-fat coconut milk
- 2 tablespoons maple syrup
- 1 tablespoon plus 1 teaspoon fresh lemon juice
- 1 teaspoon vanilla extract
- ¼ cup (35 g) unpacked dark brown sugar or coconut sugar
- 1 tablespoon coconut oil

Preparation
- Preheat the oven at 190 ° C (375 ° F). Place on medium heat a deep cast-iron skillet. Once warm, add in a single layer the apples, ½ teaspoon cinnamon, and walnuts if used. Let the apples cook while the batter is being cooked.
- In a medium bowl, combine the flour, baking powder, ¼ teaspoon salt, and ½ teaspoon cinnamon remaining. Stir the coconut milk, maple syrup, 1 tablespoon of lemon juice and vanilla together in a separate bowl, then pour

into the dry ingredients and whisk until mixed.
- Sprinkle the sugar, 1 teaspoon of lemon juice left over the apples, and 1/8 teaspoon of salt. Remove from the heat, apply the coconut oil to the pan, concentrating on the apples ' perimeter.
- Spoon the batter over the top and bake for 30 to 35 minutes, until the pancake is golden brown and cooked through. Slice into wedges, pick and serve on bowls.

Nutrition Information
Fat – 17 g
Carbohydrates – 103 g
Protein – 83 g

30. Black Bean and Veggie Soup

Serving Size: 1
Servings per Recipe: 6
Preparation Time: 10 minutes
Cooking Time: 45 minutes
Ingredients
- Olive oil - 2 tablespoons

- Onion (diced) - 1
- Celery stalks (chopped) - 2
- Carrot (chopped) - 1
- Red bell pepper (diced) - 1
- Garlic (minced) - 4 cloves
- Jalapeño (seeded and diced) - 1
- Salt - 1 teaspoon
- Pepper - 1 teaspoon
- Cumin - 2 tablespoons
- Black beans (drained and rinsed) – 4 cans (60 ounces) Vegetable stock - 4 cups
- Bay leaf – 1
- For serving
- Avocado (chopped)
- Queso fresco (crumbled)
- Fresh cilantro (chopped)
- Tortilla chip (crumbled)

Directions

1. Start by taking a stockpot (large) and place it over high flame. Add in the oil and reduce the heat the medium–high.
2. Once the oil starts to shimmer, toss in the onions, carrot, bell peppers and celery.
3. Let the veggies cook for about 5 minutes. Keep stirring.
4. Now add in the minced garlic, pepper and salt. Cook for about 10 more minutes. The veggies should be tender by now.
5. Add in the vegetable stock, black beans, bay leaf and cumin.
6. Bring the ingredients to a boil and reduce the flame to low. Cover the stockpot with a lid and cook for about 30 minutes. Beans should also be tender by now.
7. Take a blender and transfer 4 cups of the beans and vegetable soup into the same. Blend into a smooth puree like consistency.
8. Pour the blended vegetables and beans into the stockpot. Mix well to combine. This will help in thickening the soup.
9. Let the soup simmer over low flame for another 10 minutes.
10. Once done, garnish with queso fresco, avocado, tortilla chips and chopped cilantro.

Nutrition Information
Fat – 6 g
Carbohydrates – 49 g
Protein – 17 g

31. Spinach Pasta in Pesto Sauce

Serving Size: 1
Servings per Recipe: 2
Calories: 591 calories per serving

Preparation Time: 20 minutes
Cooking Time: 15 minutes

Ingredients
- Olive oil - 1 tablespoon
- Spinach - 5 ounces
- All-purpose flour - 2 cups
- Salt - 1 tablespoon plus ¼ teaspoon (keep it divided) Water - 2 tablespoons
- Roasted vegetable for serving
- Pesto for serving
- Fresh basil for serving

Directions
1. Take a large pot and fill it with water. Place it over high flame and bring the water to a boil. Add one tablespoon of salt

2. While the water is boiling, place a large saucepan over medium flame. Pour in the olive oil and heat it through.
3. Once the oil starts to shimmer, toss in the spinach and sauté for 5 minutes.
4. Take a food processor and transfer the wilted spinach. Process until the spinach is fine in texture.
5. Add in the flour bit by bit and continue to process to form a crumbly dough.
6. Further, add ¼ tsp of salt and 1 tbsp of water while processing to bring the dough together. Add the remaining 1 tbsp of water if required.
7. Remove the dough onto a flat surface and sprinkle with flour. Knead well to form a dough ball.
8. Use a rolling pin to roll out the dough. The dimensions of the rolled dough should be 18 inches long and 12 inches wide. The thickness should be about ¼ - inch thick.
9. Cut the rolled dough into long and even strips using a pizza cutter. Make sure the strips are ½ - inch wide.
10. The strips need to be rolled into evenly sized thick noodles.
11. Toss in the prepared noodles and cook for about 4 minutes. Drain using a colander.
12. Transfer the noodles into a large mixing bowl and add in the roasted vegetables, pesto. Toss well to combine.
13. Garnish with basil leaves.

Nutrition Information

Fat – 8 g

Carbohydrates – 110 g

Protein – 16 g

32. Vegan Alfredo Fettuccine Pasta

Serving Size: 1
Servings per Recipe: 2
Calories: 844 calories per serving
Preparation Time: 15 minutes
Cooking Time: 15 minutes
Ingredients
- White potatoes - 2 medium
- White onion - ¼
- Italian seasoning - 1 tablespoon
- Lemon juice - 1 teaspoon
- Garlic - 2 cloves
- Salt - 1 teaspoon
- Fettuccine pasta - 12 ounces
- Raw cashew - ½ cup
- Nutritional yeast (optional) - 1 teaspoon
- Truffle oil (optional) - ¼ teaspoon

Directions

1. Start by placing a pot on high flame and boiling 4 cups of water.
2. Peel the potatoes and cut them into small cubes. Cut the onion into cubes as well.
3. Add the potatoes and onions to the boiling water and cook for about 10 minutes.
4. Remove the onions and potatoes. Keep aside. Save the water.
5. Take another pot and fill it with water. Season generously with salt.
6. Toss in the fettuccine pasta and cook as per package instructions.
7. Take a blender and add in the raw cashews, veggies, nutritional yeast, truffle oil, lemon juice and 1 cup of saved water. Blend into a smooth puree.
8. Add in the garlic and salt.
9. Drain the cooked pasta using a colander. Transfer into a mixing bowl.
10. Pour the prepared sauce on top of the cooked fettuccine pasta. Serve.

Nutrition Information

Fat – 13 g

Carbohydrates – 152 g

Protein – 28 g

33. Tempeh Vegetarian Chili

Prep: 5 minutes
Cook: 25 minutes
Total: 30 minutes
Servings: 4

Ingredients
- 2 tablespoons of olive oil 30 mL
- 1 8-oz package tempeh 226 g, roughly grated
- 1 medium white onion diced
- 1 red bell pepper diced
- 1 stalk celery diced
- 2 cloves garlic minced
- 3/4 cup tomato sauce 177 mL
- 1 15-oz can kidney beans 425 g, drained
- 1 15-oz can black beans 425 g, drained
- 1 cup water 240 mL
- 1 tablespoon of cumin and salteach
- ¼ tablespoon of each chili powder and crushed red pepper flakes
- To serve: chopped green onions, plain Greek yogurt

Preparation

- Brown Tempeh: warm the oil in a large pot over medium / high heat. Attach the tempeh and cook for about 5 minutes until lightly browned. It's all right if some of it sticks to the pan's bottom. Once you add the fluids, it'll come off.
- Add Flavor Makers: add onion, pepper bell, celery and garlic, cook until veggies are slightly soft, about 5 minutes.
- Prepare Everything: add the remaining ingredients, reduce heat to medium, and prepare for about 15 minutes until hot and mixed. Taste the seasonings and change them as needed. Complete and serve with green onions.

Nutritional info
- Serving: 1serving
- Calories: 522kcal
- Carbohydrates: 64g
- Protein: 30g
- Fat: 22g
- Sodium: 1900mg
- Fiber: 17g

34. Healthy Lentil Soup

Total Time: 15 minutes

Number of servings: 6

Ingredients:
- 1 ½ teaspoons vegetable oil
- 2 medium carrots, sliced
- 1 ½ onions, chopped
- 1 ½ cups dry brown lentils, rinsed, soaked for about 2 hours
- 3 bay leaves
- 2 tablespoons lemon juice or to taste
- 6 cups vegetable broth
- ½ teaspoon dried thyme
- Salt to taste
- Pepper to taste

Directions:
1. Place a soup pot over medium heat. Add oil. When the oil is heated, add onions and sauté until translucent.
2. Add rest of the ingredients except lemon juice and stir.
3. When it begins to boil, lower the heat and cover with a lid. Simmer

until the lentils are tender.
4. Add lemon juice and stir.
5. Ladle into soup bowls and serve.

Nutritional values per serving: Calories – 230, Fat – 3 g, Carbohydrate – 33 g,
Fiber –15.6 g, Protein – 18.7g

35. Lentil Vegan Soup

Serving Size: 1
Servings per Recipe: 5
Calories: 364 calories per serving
Nutrition Information
Fat – 7 g
Carbohydrates – 105 g
Protein – 21 g
Preparation Time: 10 minutes
Cooking Time: 50 minutes
Ingredients
- Olive oil - 2 tablespoons
- Onion (diced) - 1
- Garlic (minced) - 2 cloves
- Carrot (diced) - 1
- Potatoes (diced) - 2
- Tomato (diced) - 1 can (15 ounces)
- Dried lentil - 2 cups

- Vegetable broth - 8 cups
- Bay leaf - 1
- Cumin - ½ teaspoon
- Salt – as per taste
- Pepper – as per taste

Directions

1. Start by taking a large pot and add in 2 tablespoons of olive oil. Place the pot over medium flame.
2. Once the oil heats through, toss in the onions and cook for 5 minutes.
3. Add in the garlic and cook for another 2 minutes.
4. Now toss in the diced potatoes and carrots. Saute for about 3 minutes.
5. Add the remaining ingredients like vegetable broth, tomatoes, lentils, cumin and bay leaf.
6. Once it comes to a boil, reduce the flame to low and cook for about 40 minutes.
7. Remove the bay leaf and season with pepper and salt.
8. Transfer into a serving bowl. Serve hot!

Nutrition Information

Fat – 7 g

Carbohydrates – 58 g

Protein – 19 g

36. Chickpea and Avocado Salad

Serving Size: 1
Servings per Recipe: 4
Calories: 399 calories per serving
Preparation Time: 15 minutes
Cooking Time: 0 minutes
Ingredients
- Dressing
- Olive oil - 2 tablespoons
- Lime juice - ¼ cup
- Cumin - 2 teaspoons
- Chili powder - 2 teaspoons
- Salt - 1 teaspoon
- Pepper - 1 teaspoon
- Fresh cilantro (chopped) - ¼ cup
- Salad
- Chickpeas (rinsed and drained) - 2 cans
- Cucumber (quartered and chopped) - 1
- Cherry tomatoes (cut in half) - 20

- Onion (chopped) - 1
- Avocado (diced) - 1
- Carrot (shredded) – 1/3 cup

Directions

1. Start by preparing the dressing. For this, take a small mixing bowl and add in the olive oil, lime juice, cumin, chili powder, salt, pepper and fresh cilantro.
2. Whisk well until all ingredients are well combined. Keep aside.
3. Take a large mixing bowl and toss in the chickpeas, tomatoes, cucumber, onion, carrots and avocado.
4. Pour the dressing over the salad and toss well using your hands or salad spoons. Ensure all ingredients are evenly combined.
5. Transfer onto salad bowl and serve!

Nutrition Information

Fat – 12 g
Carbohydrates – 57 g
Protein – 18 g

37. Roasted Vegetables and Lentil Salad

Serving Size: 1
Servings per Recipe: 2
Calories: 569 calories per serving
Preparation Time: 30 minutes
Ingredients

- Butternut squash (cubed) - 2 cups

- Brussels sprouts (quartered) - 2 cups
- Red onion (cut in wedges) - 1
- Olive oil - 1 tablespoon
- Salt – as per taste
- Pepper - as per taste
- Green lentil (rinsed) - 1 cup
- Water or vegetable broth - 3 cups
- Balsamic vinegar - 3 tablespoons
- Maple syrup - 1 tablespoon

Directions

1. Start by preheating the oven by setting the temperature to 400 degrees Fahrenheit.
2. Take a baking dish and line it with parchment paper, Toss in the butternut squash, red onions and Brussels sprouts. Generously season with salt, pepper and olive oil. Mix well using your hands and ensure all ingredients are well coated.
3. Place the tray in the baking tray in the oven and bake for 10 minutes. Flip the veggies and bake for another 10 minutes.
4. Take a medium nonstick saucepan and place it over high flame. Add in the water/vegetable broth and lentils.
5. Once it comes to a boil, cover the pan with a lid and let it simmer for about 25 minutes. Drain any excess water and keep aside.
6. Take a large mixing bowl and empty the roasted vegetables. Also transfer the cooked lentils to the mixing bowl.
7. To prepare the dressing, take a liquid measuring cup and add in the balsamic vinegar, pepper, salt and maple syrup. Whisk well to combine.
8. Pour the prepared dressing over roasted vegetables and lentil. Toss well to make sure all ingredients are well coated.
9. Transfer into 2 bowls and serve.

Nutrition Information

Fat – 8 g

Carbohydrates – 102 g

Protein – 28 g

38. Quinoa Salad Southwestern Style

Serving Size: 1
Servings per Recipe: 2
Calories: 873 calories per serving
Preparation Time: 5 minutes
Cooking Time: 22 minutes
Ingredients

- Vegetable oil - 2 tablespoons
- Garlic (minced) – 3 cloves
- Jalapeño (minced) - 1
- Black beans - 15 ounces
- Corn - 15 ounces
- Roma tomatoes (diced) - 3
- Quinoa (rinsed) - 1 cup
- Vegetable stock - 2 cups
- Chili powder - 1 tablespoon
- Cumin - 2 teaspoons
- Salt - 1 teaspoon
- Pepper - 1 teaspoon

- Avocado (cubed) - 1 teaspoon
- Lime (juiced) - 1
- Fresh cilantro (for garnishing)

Directions
1. Start by placing a large saucepan on medium flame.
2. Toss in the minced jalapeno and garlic. Cook for about a couple of minutes.
3. Add in the corn, black beans, quinoa, tomatoes, chili powder, vegetable stock, pepper and salt.
4. Cover the saucepan with the lid and cook for about 20 minutes. Quinoa should be tender and should have absorbed the liquid.
5. Mix gently using a wooden spoon.
6. Take a large serving bowl and empty the quinoa into the same. Pour lime juice and gently mix.
7. Garnish with avocado and cilantro.

Nutrition Information
Fat – 23 g
Carbohydrates – 143 g
Protein – 33 g

39. Easy bean burritos

Preparation time: 3 minutes
Cooking time: 1 minute
Number of servings: 2

Ingredients
- 1½ cups (390 g) Slow-Cooker Refried Beans
- 1 large sweet potato, cubed and roasted or steamed
- ½ cup (30 g) nutritional yeast
- ½ cup (120 g) salsa 12 (8-inch or 20 cm) wholegrain tortillas
- 1 cup (245 g) hummus or 1 cup (240 ml)

Direction

• Drain from the sautéed vegetables some excess liquid. In a pan, add the peas, sautéed onions, sweet potatoes, nutritional yeast and salsa. Put it aside.

• Using tortillas, hummus, bean mixture and 12 pieces of parchment paper or aluminum foil to set up an assembly line on the fridge.

• Warm the tortillas one at a time. (Microwave them for about 15 seconds each, or bake them for 5 to 7 minutes at 350 ° F/180 ° C wrapped in a wet, lint-free towel.)

• Lay hummus on a hot tortilla, then top with ½ cup (90 g) of bean-vegetable mixture. Roll, first pull the bottom and top in, then the sides in. Wrap the parchment or foil securely. Continue and top with the leftover tortillas. Enable cooling, then cooling for up to 5 days or freezing for up to 2 months.

Nutrition Information

Fat – 12g

Carbohydrates – 63 g

Protein – 33 g

40. Sweet Potato, Spinach & Butter Bean Stew

Servings: 12 (can easily by halved)
Ready in: 45 Minutes
Ingredients
- 1.25 kg sweet potatoes
- 260g young leaf spinach
- 4 x 400g can chopped tomatoes
- 2 x 400g can butter beans
- 4 garlic cloves (crushed)
- 2 medium onions (finely chopped)
- 2 tablespoons of olive oil
- 2 tablespoons of ground cumin
- 2 tablespoons of ground coriander
- 3 tablespoons of smoked paprika
- 500ml vegetable stock
- Juice of 1 to 2 lemons
- Large bunch of fresh coriander
- Salt & pepper

Preparation
- Cut and slice sweet potatoes in 1 cm dice (0.40 inch).
- In a large pot, warm olive oil.

- Fine-cut onion, split garlic, ground cumin, ground coriander, and smoked paprika. Cook until tender is the onion.
- Include sweet potatoes, tomatoes chopped, and stock.
- Take to the boil and cook until sweet potatoes are soft (they should still have a bite).
- Cut the spinach. Cook for about 2 minutes. Add butter beans that have been rinsed and drained. Cook to warm them up for another 2 minutes.
- Season with lemon juice, salt, and pepper to taste.
- Serve with plenty of fresh ground leaves of chopped coriander.

Nutrition Information

Fat – 19 g

Carbohydrates – 43 g

Protein – 23 g

Chapter 10: Soup Recipes

41. Tofu and mushroom soup

Total Time: 25 minutes | Servings: 4

Ingredients:

2 tbsp olive oil
1 garlic clove, minced
1 large yellow onion, finely chopped
1 tsp freshly grated ginger
1 cup vegetable stock
2 small potatoes, peeled and chopped
¼ tsp salt
¼ tsp black pepper
2 (14 oz) silken tofu, drained and rinsed
2/3 cup baby Bella mushrooms, sliced
1 tbsp chopped fresh oregano
2 tbsp chopped fresh parsley to garnish

Direction

Heat the olive oil in a medium pot over medium heat and sauté the garlic, onion, and ginger until soft and fragrant.

Pour in the vegetable stock, potatoes, salt, and black pepper. Cook until the

potatoes soften, 12 minutes.
Stir in the tofu and using an immersion blender, puree the ingredients until smooth.
Mix in the mushrooms and simmer with the pot covered until the mushrooms warm up while occasionally stirring to ensure that the tofu doesn't curdle, 7 minutes.
Stir oregano, and dish the soup.
Garnish with the parsley and serve warm.

Nutritional values per serving: Calories – 156, Fat – 3 g, Carbohydrate – 23 g,
Fiber –16 g, Protein – 17g

42. Avocado green soup

Total Time: 10 minutes | Servings: 4
Ingredients:
2 tbsp olive oil
1 ½ cup fresh kale, chopped coarsely
1 ½ cup fresh spinach, chopped coarsely
3 large avocados, halved, pitted and pulp extracted
2 cups of soy milk
2 cups no-sodium vegetable broth

3 tbsp chopped fresh mint leaves
¼ tsp salt

- ¼ tsp black pepper
- 2 limes, juiced

Direction
1. Heat the olive oil in a medium saucepan over medium heat and mix in the kale and spinach. Cook until wilted, 3 minutes and turn off the heat.
2. Add the remaining ingredients and using an immersion blender, puree the soup until smooth.
3. Dish the soup and serve immediately.
Nutritional values per serving: Calories – 100, Fat – 5 g, Carbohydrate – 13 g,
Fiber –26 g, Protein – 14g

43. Spicy Black Bean Soup

Total Time: 15 minutes
Number of servings: 4
Ingredients:
- 1 large onion, finely chopped
- 2 tablespoons olive oil
- 2 jalapeño peppers, deseeded, minced
- 2 red bell peppers, chopped
- 2 cups vegetable broth
- 3 teaspoons freshly ground cumin
- 2 tablespoons balsamic vinegar
- 1 Hungarian pepper, deseeded, minced
- 4 cloves garlic, minced
- 2 cans (15 ounces each) black beans
- 1 avocado, peeled, pitted, chopped
- Salt to taste
- Pepper to taste
- 2 tablespoons fresh cilantro, chopped
- 4 tortillas

Directions:
1. Mash about 1 can of black beans. Add garlic to it and stir. Set aside.
2. Place a heavy-bottomed pot over medium heat. Add oil. When the oil is heated, add onions, peppers (all the varieties) and cumin and sauté until the vegetables are soft.
3. Add rest of the ingredients except cilantro and bring to a boil.
4. Ladle into soup bowls and serve hot garnished with cilantro.

Nutritional values per serving: Calories – 536, Fat – 22 g, Carbohydrate – 65 g,
Fiber – 20 g, Protein – 21 g

44. Red Curry Quinoa Soup

Total Time: 30 minutes
Number of servings: 3
Ingredients:
- ½ tablespoon olive oil
- 1 small green bell pepper, deseeded, chopped
- 1 medium yellow onion, chopped
- 1 small sweet potato, chopped (about ¾ cup)
- ½ tablespoon red curry paste
- ½ cup quinoa
- 1 tablespoon lime juice
- A handful fresh cilantro, chopped

- 1 clove garlic, chopped
- 1 teaspoon fresh ginger, peeled, chopped
- 2 cups vegetable broth or water
- Salt to taste

Directions:
1. Place a pot over medium-high heat. Add oil. When the oil is heated, add onion, sweet potato and bell pepper.
2. Sauté for about 10 minutes.
3. Stir in ginger, garlic and curry paste. Sauté until aromatic.
4. Add quinoa and stir-fry for a minute.
5. Add broth and stir.
6. When it begins to boil, lower the heat and cook until sweet potatoes and quinoa are cooked.
7. Turn off the heat. Stir in lime juice and salt.
8. Ladle into soup bowls. Sprinkle cilantro on top and serve.

Nutritional values per serving: Calories – 164, Fat – 4 g, Carbohydrate – 26 g,
Fiber – NA, Protein – 6 g

45. Split Pea Soup

Total Time: 20 minutes
Number of servings: 3
Ingredients:
- ½ tablespoon canola oil
- 1 medium white onion, finely chopped
- 1 small stalk celery, sliced
- 2 cups vegetable broth
- ¾ cups green split peas, rinsed
- ½ small russet potato, cubed
- ½ teaspoon ground cumin
- Freshly ground pepper to taste
- 1 cup water
- Salt to taste
- 1 small carrot, chopped

Directions:
1. Place a soup pot over medium heat. Add oil. When the oil is heated, add onion, garlic, celery, and carrots and sauté for 3-4 minutes.
2. Add rest of the ingredients in a large pot and stir.

3. Cook until the split peas and potatoes are tender. Add more water if required.
4. Mix well. Ladle into soup bowls and serve hot.

Nutritional values per serving: Calories – 163, Fat – 3 g, Carbohydrate – 29 g,
Fiber – 5 g, Protein – 7 g

46. Tofu Noodle Soup

Total Time: 15 minutes
Number of servings: 8
Ingredients:
- 1 large head broccoli, cut into florets
- 2 blocks (14 ounces each) firm tofu, drained, pressed of excess moisture
- 2 teaspoons coconut oil
- 3 tablespoons olive oil
- 2 cups diced celery
- 2 cups chopped carrots
- 2 large onions, thinly sliced
- ¼ teaspoon black pepper
- ¼ teaspoon white pepper
- 4 tablespoons soy sauce

- 3 tablespoons rice vinegar (optional)
- 1 teaspoon red chili flakes
- 2 tablespoons nutritional yeast
- Salt to taste
- 16 ounces brown rice elbow pasta

Directions:
1. Spread the tofu cubes on a lined baking sheet.
2. Bake in a preheated oven at 400° F until light brown.
3. Place a large pot over medium-high heat. Add coconut oil and olive oil. When it is heated, add celery, onion and carrot and sauté for about 4-5 minutes.
4. Add garlic, and all the spices. Sauté for a few seconds until aromatic.
5. Add tofu, pasta, and broccoli and stir-fry for a couple of minutes.
6. Add the rest of the ingredients and cook pasta until is al dente.
7. Ladle into soup bowls and serve.

Nutritional values per serving: Calories – 404, Fat – 13 g, Carbohydrate – 55 g, Fiber – 5 g, Protein – 17 g

47. Hot and Sour Soup

Total Time: 15 minutes
Number of servings: 8
Ingredients:
- 8 cloves garlic, minced
- 4 tablespoons grated ginger, divided
- 2 packages (10 ounces each) mushrooms, sliced
- 16 fresh shiitake mushrooms, sliced
- 2 cans (8 ounces each) bamboo shoots, drained, julienned
- 2 package (15 ounces each) firm or silken tofu, chopped into small cubes
- 3 cups frozen peas
- 8 cups water
- 4 tablespoons vegan chicken-flavored bouillon
- 2 teaspoons chili paste
- 4 tablespoons soy sauce or tamari
- 4 tablespoons rice wine vinegar
- 2 teaspoons sesame oil + extra to drizzle

Directions:
1. Add all the ingredients except half the ginger and peas into a soup pot.
2. Place the pot over medium heat. When it begins to boil, lower the heat and cook until slightly tender. Stir occasionally.

3. Add peas and half the ginger and stir. Cook for a minute.
4. Cover and let it sit for 5 minutes. Taste and adjust the seasoning if required.
5. Ladle into soup bowls and serve.

Nutritional values per serving: Calories – 208, Fat – 7.4 g, Carbohydrate – 21.6 g,
Fiber – 5.4 g, Protein – 19.2 g

48. Spicy SunDried Tomato Soup with White Beans & Swiss Chard

Total Time: 20 minutes
Number of servings: 4
Ingredients:
- 1 tablespoon olive oil
- ¼ teaspoon red pepper flakes
- 1 medium carrot, sliced
- ½ small zucchini, sliced

- ¾ cup chopped onion
- 1 stalk celery, chopped
- 1 teaspoon minced fresh rosemary
- 1 can (15 ounces) diced tomatoes
- ¼ cup oil-packed sundried tomatoes, drained, chopped
- 1 tablespoon oil from oil packed sun-drained tomatoes
- ¼ teaspoon chopped thyme
- 2 cloves garlic, minced
- 1 cup vegetable broth
- ½ can (from a 15 ounces can) white beans or cannellini beans, rinsed, drained
- 3 ounces Swiss chard, chopped
- ½ cup torn basil

Directions:

1. Place a soup pot over medium heat. Add oil. When the oil is heated, add garlic and red pepper flakes and sauté until aromatic.
2. Add onion, carrots, zucchini, celery, and rosemary and sauté until onions turn translucent.
3. Stir in the broth, beans, and ½ can tomatoes. Mix well. Add some of the mixture into the blender. Add rest of the canned tomatoes, sundried tomatoes, and its oil and blend until smooth.
4. Pour it back into the pot.
5. Heat thoroughly. Add salt and pepper to taste. Let it simmer for a few minutes. Garnish with basil and serve.
6. Ladle into soup bowls.

Nutritional values per serving: Calories – 169, Fat – 8 g, Carbohydrate – 21 g,
Fiber – 6 g, Protein – 5 g

49. Lentil Spinach Soup

Total Time: 5 minutes
Number of servings: 8
Ingredients:
- 4 cups vegetable broth
- 1 teaspoon ground cumin
- Salt to taste
- Pepper to taste
- ½ cup water
- 6 tablespoons olive oil
- 2 whole carrots, peeled, chopped
- 2 tablespoons tomato paste
- ½ teaspoon smoked paprika
- ½ cup + 2 tablespoons dry lentils, green or brown or red, rinse
- 4 cups chopped spinach
- Juice of a lemon
- 1 medium onion, chopped
- 2-3 cloves garlic, minced
- 1 bay leaf

Directions:
1. Place a saucepan or soup pot over medium heat. Add oil. When the oil is heated, add onion and carrot and sauté until the onions are translucent.
2. Add garlic, paprika, cumin, and salt and sauté for a few seconds until fragrant.
3. Stir in the tomato paste and pepper and cook for a couple of minutes.

4. Add water, lentils, and broth and bring to the boil.
5. Lower the heat and cover with a lid. Simmer until the lentils are tender. Add more water or broth if required.
6. Add spinach and cook until spinach wilts. Turn off the heat. Add lemon juice and stir. Taste and add more seasonings or lemon juice if required.
7. Ladle into soup bowls and serve.

Nutritional values per serving: Calories – 354, Fat – 12 g, Carbohydrate – 41 g,
Fiber – 18 g, Protein – 21 g

50. Potato, Bean and Kale Soup

Total Time: 15 minutes
Number of servings: 3
Ingredients:
- 1 cup chopped onion
- 4 cups vegetable broth
- 1 can (15 ounces) pinto beans, drained or 1 ½ cups cooked pinto beans
- 3 cloves garlic, minced
- ½ pound small potatoes, chopped into bite-sized pieces
- 5 -6 cups chopped kale leaves, discard hard stems and ribs
- ½ teaspoon dried basil
- ½ teaspoon dried oregano
- ¼ teaspoon dried rosemary, crushed

- ¼ teaspoons red pepper flakes
- ¼ teaspoon fennel seeds
- ¼ cup nondairy milk of your choice (optional)
- 1 tablespoon nutritional yeast
- Salt to taste
- Pepper to taste

Directions:
1. Add all the ingredients except kale, milk, and nutritional yeast into a soup pot.
2. Place the pot over medium heat. Cover and cook until potatoes are tender.
3. Add kale and stir. Cover and cook for 5-8 minutes until kale is bright green in color and tender as well.
4. Add milk and nutritional yeast. Mix well.
5. Taste and adjust the seasoning if necessary.
6. Ladle into soup bowls and serve.

Nutritional values per serving: Calories – 207, Fat – 1.3 g, Carbohydrate – 39.9 g,
Fiber – 8.5 g, Protein – 11.1 g

Chapter 11: Salad Recipes

51. Mexican Street Salad

Total Time: 10 minutes
Number of servings: 5
Ingredients:
- 5 medium radishes, trimmed, finely sliced
- 1 small white cabbage, shredded
- ¼ small red cabbage, shredded
- ¼ cup extra-virgin olive oil
- 4 carrots, peeled, finely sliced
- Handful cilantro, finely chopped
- 4 large jalapeno chilies or to taste, finely sliced
- 2 red onions, peeled, finely sliced
- ½ cup lime juice
- Sea salt to taste

Directions:

1. Add all the ingredients in a bowl except the red cabbage. Toss well.
2. Add the red cabbage just before serving.

Nutritional values per serving: Calories – 111, Fat – 6.5 g, Carbohydrate – 9.24 g,
Fiber – 4.2 g, Protein – 2.2 g

52. Mediterranean Bean Salad

Total Time: 15 minutes
Number of servings: 3
Ingredients:
- ½ can (from a 15 ounce can) black beans, drained, rinsed
- ½ can (from a 15.5 ounce can chickpeas, drained, rinsed
- 1 clove garlic, peeled, minced
- 2 tablespoons chopped fresh mint
- 2 tablespoons chopped fresh parsley
- ½ cup chopped grape tomatoes
- ¼ cup chopped red onion
- Juice of ½ lemon
- 2 teaspoons olive oil
- Freshly ground pepper to taste
- Kosher salt to taste

Directions:
1. Add olive oil and lemon juice to a small bowl and whisk until emulsified.

2. Add all the rest of the ingredients into a bowl and toss well.
3. Pour dressing over it. Toss well and set aside for 30 minutes at room temperature.
4. Toss again and serve.

Nutritional values per serving: Calories – 175, Fat – 4.5 g, Carbohydrate – 26 g, Fiber – 9 g, Protein – 8 g

53. Strawberry Spinach Salad with Avocado & Walnuts

Total Time: 25 minutes
Number of servings: 2
Ingredients:
- 6 cups baby spinach
- 1 cup sliced strawberries
- ½ medium avocado, diced
- 2 tablespoons finely chopped red onion
- 4 tablespoons vinaigrette
- 4 tablespoons toasted walnut pieces

Directions:

1. Add onion, strawberries, and spinach into a bowl and toss well.
2. Pour vinaigrette and toss well.
3. Scatter walnuts and avocado on top and serve.

Nutritional values per serving: Calories – 296, Fat – 18 g, Carbohydrate – 27 g,
Fiber – 10 g, Protein – 8 g

54. Black Bean and Corn Salad

Total Time: 10 minutes
Number of servings: 8
Ingredients:
- 2 cans (15 ounces each) black beans, drained, rinsed
- ½ cup red onion, finely chopped
- 1 red bell pepper, chopped
- 1 yellow bell pepper, chopped
- 2 cups fresh corn kernels
- 1 large avocado, peeled, pitted, chopped

- 2 small tomatoes, chopped
- ½ cup fresh cilantro, chopped
- 4 scallions, chopped
- Salt to taste
- Pepper to taste
- Juice of 2 limes
- 2 teaspoons dried basil
- 2 teaspoons dried oregano
- 1 teaspoon ground cumin

Directions:
1. Add all the ingredients into a bowl and toss well.
2. Cover and set aside for a while for the flavors to set in.

Nutritional values per serving: Calories – 154, Fat – 1 g, Carbohydrate – 30.9 g, Fiber – 9.8 g, Protein – 7.8 g

55. Pineapple & Avocado Salad

Total Time: 30 minutes

Number of servings: 4

Ingredients:
- 1 medium red onion, sliced into thin rounds
- 1 firm, ripe avocado, peeled, pitted, chopped
- 1 ½ tablespoons extra-virgin olive oil
- ½ tablespoon fresh lime juice

- Freshly ground pepper to taste
- Salt to taste
- 1 small fresh ripe pineapple, skinned, cored, chopped
- Ice water, as required

Directions:
1. Add onions into a bowl of ice water. Let it remain in it for 15 minutes. Drain.
2. To make the dressing: Add oil and lime juice into a bowl. Whisk well.
3. Place the avocado, pineapple, and onions in any manner you desire, on a serving plate. Sprinkle salt.
4. Pour dressing over it. Sprinkle pepper and serve.

Nutritional values per serving: Calories – 186, Fat – 13 g, Carbohydrate – 20 g, Fiber – 5 g, Protein – 2 g

56. Edamame and Chickpeas Salad

Total Time: 10 minutes
Number of servings: 4
Ingredients:
- 1 cup shelled edamame
- 3 tablespoons minced red onion
- 3 tablespoons minced carrots
- 1 cup cooked chickpeas
- 3 tablespoons minced red bell pepper
- 2 tablespoons dried sweetened cranberries
- 2 tablespoons sunflower seeds
- 3 tablespoons olive oil
- 3 tablespoons apple cider vinegar
- Celery salt to taste
- 3 tablespoons agave nectar
- 1 tablespoon vegan mayonnaise – refer Chapter: Vegan Sauces
- A pinch cayenne pepper or to taste

Directions:
1. Add all of the ingredients into a bowl and toss well.
2. Serve.

Nutritional values per serving: Calories – 333, Fat – 16.8 g, Carbohydrate – 37.1 g,

Fiber – 5.9 g, Protein – 11.5 g

57. Black and White Bean Quinoa Salad

Total Time: 15 minutes
Number of servings: 2
Ingredients:
For the salad:
- 3 tablespoons quinoa
- ½ can (from a 15 ounces can) navy beans, drained, rinsed
- ½ can (from a 15 ounces can) black beans, drained, rinsed
- 1 small red onion, chopped
- 1 small cucumber, chopped
- 2 tablespoons chopped fresh cilantro
- 1 small jalapeño, deseeded, chopped (optional)

For the dressing:
- 2 tablespoons vegetable oil
- ½ tablespoon apple cider vinegar
- ¼ teaspoon chili powder
- ¼ teaspoon dried oregano
- Pepper to taste

- Salt to taste
- ½ teaspoon ground coriander
- 1 small clove garlic, minced
- 1 tablespoon lime juice

Directions:

1. To make the dressing: Add all the ingredients of the dressing into a bowl. Whisk well. Set aside for a while for the flavors to set in.
2. Cook quinoa following the instructions on the package but add a bit of salt while cooking. Set aside.
3. Add salad ingredients into a bowl. Add cooked quinoa and toss well.
4. Pour dressing on top. Toss well and serve.

Nutritional values per serving: Calories – 415, Fat – 16 g, Carbohydrate – 55 g, Fiber – NA, Protein – 17 g

58. Tempeh Salad

Total Time: 20 minutes

Number of servings: 4

Ingredients:

- 2 cups tempeh, cubed, steamed, cooled
- 2 sticks celery, chopped
- 1 onion, chopped
- 2 medium pickles, chopped
- ¼ cup parsley, minced
- 1 ½ tablespoons soy sauce

- 1 cup vegan mayonnaise
- 2 cloves garlic minced
- 4 teaspoons mustard
- 3-4 teaspoons curry powder (optional)

Directions:
1. Add all the ingredients to a large bowl. Toss well.
2. Chill for a couple of hours and serve.

Nutritional values per serving: Calories – 248.9, Fat – 14.1 g, Carbohydrate – 18 g,
Fiber – 1.5 g, Protein – 17.1 g

59. Edamame Salad

Total Time: 15 minutes
Number of servings: 4
Ingredients:
- ½ pound frozen edamame, shelled, cooked according to the instructions on the package, drained, rinsed
- ½ red bell pepper, deseeded, chopped

- 1 ½ cups frozen corn kernels
- 1 cup red onions, sliced
- 2 green onions, sliced
- 1 tablespoon chopped fresh oregano or basil
- 2 tablespoons chopped parsley

For dressing:
- 3 tablespoons lemon juice
- 1 tablespoon olive oil
- 1 tablespoon Dijon mustard
- Pepper to taste
- Salt to taste

Directions:
1. To make the dressing: Whisk together all the ingredients of the dressing.
2. Add all of the ingredients to a large bowl and toss well. Pour dressing on top. Toss well. Chill until use.

Nutritional values per serving: Calories – 240.4, Fat – 8.5 g, Carbohydrate – 35.9 g,
Fiber – 6.5 g, Protein – 11.8 g

60. White bean and tomato salad

Total Time: 15 minutes | Servings: 4
Ingredients:

For the dressing:

- 3 tbsp freshly squeezed lemon juice
- ¼ cup olive oil
- 1 garlic clove, minced
- ¼ tsp salt
- 1/8 tsp black pepper

For the salad:

- 2 (15 oz) cans white beans, drained and rinsed
- 2 cups cherry tomatoes, quartered
- ½ small red onion, sliced
- 1 garlic clove, minced
- ½ cup chopped fresh parsley

Direction
1. Mix the dressing's ingredients in a large bowl until well-combined and add the white beans, garlic, tomatoes, onion, and parsley.
2. Coat the salad with the dressing.
3. Serve immediately.

Nutritional values per serving: Calories – 124, Fat – 4g, Carbohydrate – 5.9 g,
Fiber – 8 g, Protein – 7 g

61. Tofu Bean Salad

Cook time: 15 minutes Servings: 4

Ingredients
- 12 slices Tofu Bacon, cut into pieces
- 1 can black beans, drained
- 1 large head romaine lettuce, washed, chopped
- 1 avocado, sliced
- 1 can organic corn

- 24 cherry tomatoes
- ½ cup cilantro, chopped
- Fresh lime juice, for dressing

Instructions
1. Divide all the ingredients between 4 plates and drizzle with lime juice dressing.
2. Toss well to combined. Enjoy immediately.

Nutrition Values:
Calories: 78
Protein: 15g
Fat: 7 g
Carbs: 18g
Fibers: 9g

62. Quinoa Salad

Time: 25 Minutes
Servings: Four
Ingredients:
- Sunflower Seeds (.50 C.)
- Sun Died Tomatoes (.25 C.)
- Parsley (.25 C.)
- Fresh Dill (.25 C.)
- Lemon (1)

- Chickpeas (1 Can)
- Broccoli Florets (3 C.)
- Red Onion (.25 C.)
- Olive Oil (2 T.)
- Dry Quinoa (1 C.)

Directions:

1. To start this recipe, you will first want to cook your quinoa according to the directions included on the package.

2. Once the quinoa is cooked through, you can bring a skillet over medium heat. Once the pan is warm, pour in the olive oil and bring the oil to a gentle sizzle. At this point, you will now add in the broccoli and red onion. When the vegetables are in place, cook them for five minutes or until they are both soft.

3. Next, you will want to take a large salad bowl and place your quinoa, dill, parsley, sun-dried tomatoes, chickpeas, red onion, and the cooked broccoli.

4. For extra flavor, squeeze the juice of one lemon over everything in the bowl. Once this is done, give the salad a toss, season with salt and pepper, and enjoy your meal!

Nutrition Values:
Calories: 460
Protein: 17g
Fat: 19g
Carbs: 62g
Fibers: 13g

63. Thai Zucchini Noodle Salad

Time: 25 Minutes
Servings: Four
Ingredients:
- Peanuts (.50 C.)
- Peanut Sauce (.50 C.)
- Water (2 T.)
- Extra-firm Tofu (.50 Block)
- Chopped Green Onions (.25 C.)
- Spiralized Carrot (1)
- Spiralized Zucchini (3)

Directions:

1. First, you are going to want to create your peanut sauce. To do this, take a small bowl and slowly mix your peanut sauce with water. You will want to add one tablespoon at a time to achieve the thickness you desire.

2. Next, you will combine all of the ingredients from above, minus the peanuts, into a large mixing bowl. Once everything is in place, top with the salad dressing and give everything a good toss to assure even coating.

3. Finally, sprinkle your peanuts on top, and your meal is done!

Nutrition Values:

Calories: 200

Protein: 13g

Fat: 13g

Carbs: 11g

Fibers: 5g

64. Bacon & Broccoli Salad

Preparation Time: 15 minutes Cooking Time: 0 minute Servings: 6

Ingredients:
- ¼ cup light mayonnaise
- 1 clove garlic, crushed and minced
- 2 teaspoons cider vinegar
- 1 teaspoon sugar
- ¼ cup low-fat sour cream
- 4 cups broccoli, chopped
- 8 oz. water chestnuts, rinsed, drained and chopped
- 3 tablespoons dried cranberries
- 3 slices turkey bacon, cooked and crumbled
- Pepper to taste

Method:
1. Combine the mayo, garlic, vinegar, sugar and sour cream in a bowl.
2. Toss the broccoli, water chestnuts, cranberries and bacon in the dressing.
3. Season with the pepper.
4. Refrigerate for up to 1 day.

Nutritional Value:
- Calories: 92
- Total fat: 4.5g
- Saturated fat: 1.5g
- Cholesterol: 10mg
- Sodium: 160mg
- Potassium: 191mg
- Carbohydrates: 10.8g
- Fiber: 1.9g
- Sugar: 4g
- Protein: 3.3g

65. Green Curry Tofu

Time: 1 Hour

Servings: Four

Ingredients:
- Lime Juice (1 T.)
- Tamari Sauce (1 T.)
- Water Chestnuts (8 Oz.)
- Green Beans (1 C.)
- Salt (.50 t.)
- Vegetable Broth (.50 C.)
- Coconut Milk (14 Oz.)
- Chickpeas (1 C.)
- Green Curry Paste (3 T.)
- Frozen Edamame (1 C.)
- Garlic Cloves (2)
- Ginger (1 inch)
- Olive Oil (1 t.)
- Diced Onion (1)
- Extra-firm Tofu (8 Oz.)
- Brown Basmati Rice (1 C.)

Directions:
1. To start, you will want to cook your rice according to the directions on the package. You can do this in a rice cooker or simply on top of the stove.
2. Next, you will want to prepare your tofu. You can remove the tofu from the package and set it on a plate. Once in place, set another plate on top and something heavy so you can begin to drain the tofu. Once the tofu is prepared, cut it into half inch cubes.
3. Next, take a medium-sized pan and place it over medium heat. As the pan heats up, go ahead and place your olive oil. When the olive oil begins to sizzle, add your onions and cook until they turn a nice translucent color. Typically, this process will take about five minutes. When your onions are ready, add in the garlic and ginger. With these in place, cook the ingredients for another two to three minutes.
4. Once the last step is done, add in your curry paste and edamame. Cook these two ingredients until the edamame is no longer frozen.
5. With these ready, you will now add in the cubed tofu, chickpeas, vegetable broth, coconut milk, and the salt. When everything is in place, you will want to bring the pot to a simmer. Add in the water chestnuts and green beans next and cook for a total of five minutes.
6. When all of the ingredients are cooked through, you can remove the pan from the heat and divide your meal into bowls. For extra flavor, try stirring in tamari, lime juice, or soy sauce. This recipe is excellent served over rice or any other side dish!

Nutrition Values:
Calories: 760
Protein: 23g
Fat: 38g
Carbs: 89g
Fibers: 9g

66. Fruit Salad

Preparation Time: 20 minutes Cooking Time: 0 minute Servings: 6

Ingredients:

- 8 oz. cream cheese
- 1 tablespoon honey
- 6 oz. Greek yogurt
- 1 teaspoon orange zest
- 1 teaspoon lemon zest
- 1 orange, sliced into sections
- 3 kiwi, sliced
- 1 mango, cubed
- 1 cup fresh blueberries

Direction:

1. Beat the cream cheese using an electric mixer.
2. Stir in the honey, yogurt, orange zest and lemon zest.
3. In a glass jar with lid, arrange the fruits in layers.

4. Top with the cream cheese mixture.
5. Seal the jar and refrigerate for up to 1 day.

Nutritional Value:
Calories: 153
Total fat: 19 g
Saturated fat: 3g
Sodium: 211mg
Potassium: 539mg
Carbohydrates: 31g
Fiber: 5g
Sugar: 7g
Protein: 5g

67. Berry salad with Arugula

Time: 10 minutes | Servings: 4

Ingredients:
For the dressing:
1 ½ cups fresh raspberry
¼ cup red wine vinegar
1 tsp Dijon mustard
1/8 tsp black pepper
½ cup olive oil
1 tbsp. spirinula
1 small shallot, diced
For the salad:
6 cups arugula
½ cup blueberries
1 cup strawberries, halved
½ cup raspberries
1/3 cup red onion, thinly sliced
1/3 cup goat cheese, crumbled
¼ cup walnuts, roughly chopped

Direction
1. Add all the dressings ingredients into a food processor and blend until smooth. Set aside.
2. Spread the arugula in the bottom of a wide salad bowl and top with the remaining ingredients.
3. Drizzle the dressing on top, toss well, and enjoy immediately.
Calories – 386, Fat – 9 g, Carbohydrate – 65 g, Fiber – 19 g, Protein – 23 g

68. Grilled tempeh and chickpea salad

Time: 5 minutes | Servings: 4

Ingredients:

- 4 tempeh fillets, grilled and chopped
- 2 (15 oz) cans chickpeas, drained and rinsed
- 1 tbsp drained capers
- 1 red onion, thinly sliced
- 2 tbsp olive oil
- 1 tbsp red wine vinegar
- A pinch salt
- 1/8 tsp black pepper

Direction
1. In a salad bowl, mix the tempeh, chickpeas, capers, and onion.
2. In a small bowl, whisk the olive oil, vinegar, salt, and black pepper. Drizzle the mixture on the salad and toss well.
3. Serve immediately.

Calories – 126, Fat – 6 g, Carbohydrate – 62 g, Fiber – 9 g, Protein – 20 g

69. Zucchini fennel salad

Total Time: 17 minutes | Servings: 4

Ingredients:

- 2 lb. zucchinis cut into ½-inch cubes
- 2 tbsp vegan butter
- Salt and black pepper to taste
- 2 oz. chopped scallions
- 3 oz. fennel, greenside sliced finely
- 1 cup vegan mayonnaise
- 2 tbsp fresh chives, finely chopped
- A pinch mustard powder
- Chopped dill to garnish

Direction

1. Heat the vegan butters in a medium skillet over medium heat and sauté the zucchinis until slightly softened but not browned, 7 minutes.
2. Turn off the heat, pour the zucchinis into a salad bowl and allow cooling.

3. Mix in the scallions, fennel, vegan mayonnaise, chives, and mustard powder.
4. Garnish with dill and serve.

Calories – 129, Fat – 16 g, Carbohydrate – 67.2 g, Fiber – 19 g, Protein – 23 g

70. Vegan Greek salad

Total Time: 10 minutes | Servings: 2

Ingredients:

- For the salad:
- ½ yellow bell pepper, seeded and cut into bite-size pieces
- ½ red onion, peeled and sliced thinly
- ½ cup tofu cheese, cut into bite-size squares
- 10 Kalamata olives pitted
- 3 large tomatoes cut into bite-size pieces
- ½ cucumber, cut into bite-size pieces
- For the dressing:

- 4 tbsp olive oil
- ½ tbsp red wine vinegar
- 2 tsp dried oregano
- Salt and black pepper to taste

Direction
1. In a salad bowl, combine all the salad's ingredients until well combined
2. In a small bowl, mix the dressing's ingredients and toss into the salad.
3. Dish the salad and enjoy!

Calories – 326, Fat – 26 g, Carbohydrate – 72 g, Fiber – 13 g, Protein – 21 g

Chapter 12: Dinner Recipes

71. Vegan Greek Meatball Soup

Preparation time: 10 minutes
Cooking time: 50 – 60 minutes
Number of servings: 4
Nutrition facts per serving:
Ingredients:
- ¾ cup dry brown lentils, rinsed, soaked in water for a couple of hours if possible
- ½ small onion, chopped
- 2 ½ cups vegetable broth
- Juice of a large lemon
- 2 tablespoons breadcrumbs
- Salt to taste
- Pepper to taste
- 7 tablespoons long grain brown rice
- ¼ cup flour
- ½ tablespoon cornstarch mixed with 2 tablespoons water
- 2 tablespoons chopped parsley
- 1 tablespoon olive oil

- 1 tablespoon ground flaxseeds
- 2 cups water
- ¼ cup flour
- Olive oil, to drizzle

Directions:

1. Place a saucepan over medium-high heat. Add 2 cups broth and lentils into saucepan.
2. When it begins to boil, reduce the heat to medium heat and simmer until lentils are cooked. Place a wire mesh strainer over a bowl and strain the lentils. Retain the cooked water.
3. Place another small saucepan with 6 tablespoons rice and remaining broth over medium heat. Cook until rice is soft. Turn off the heat.
4. Add the retained lentil cooked liquid back to the saucepan. Add water and place over medium heat.
5. Meanwhile, add lentils and half the cooked into the food processor bowl and pulse until coarsely mashed.
6. Transfer into a bowl. Add remaining cooked rice, parsley, oil, breadcrumbs and flaxseeds and mix until well combined.
7. Divide the mixture 12 equal portions and shape into balls. Place flour on a plate. Dredge the balls in flour.
8. Add remaining tablespoon of uncooked rice to the simmering broth and drop the lentil balls into it.
9. Reduce heat and simmer for about 30 minutes.
10. Add cornstarch mixture to the simmering broth and stir gently. Add lemon juice, salt and pepper and mix well.
11. Ladle into soup bowls. Trickle some olive oil on top and serve.

Calories – 461.8, Fat – 5.75 g, Carbohydrate – 51.6 g, Fiber – NA, Protein – 20 g

72. Irish "Lamb" Stew

Preparation time: 10 minutes
Cooking time: 50 – 60 minutes
Number of servings: 4
Nutrition facts per serving:
Ingredients:
- ½ cup Textured vegetable protein (TVP) chunks or soy chunks
- Salt to taste
- Pepper to taste
- 3 cloves garlic, minced
- 2 stalks celery, chopped
- 2 potatoes, peeled, chopped into chunks
- 1 ½ - 2 ½ cups vegetable stock
- ½ tablespoon minced fresh rosemary
- 2 tablespoons all-purpose flour
- 1 medium onion, chopped
- 1 cup button mushrooms or crimini mushrooms, halved or quartered depending on the size of the mushrooms
- 1 medium carrot, cut into thin, round slices
- ¼ bottle beer or ¼ cup wine
- ½ tablespoon minced, fresh thyme
- 1 tablespoon vegetable oil

Directions:
1. Add TVP into a bowl of hot water and let it soak for 30-40 minutes. Drain and set aside for 5-7 minutes.
2. Add flour, salt and pepper into a bowl and stir. Roll the TVP chunks in

the flour mixture. Shake the chunks to drop off extra flour. Set aside the remaining flour mixture.
3. Place a soup pot over medium heat. Add 2 teaspoons oil and heat.
4. Add TVP and stir. Cook until brown all over.
5. Remove with a slotted spoon and place on a plate lined with paper towels.
6. Add ½ teaspoon oil into the pot. When the oil is heated, add garlic, salt, pepper and onion and sauté until onions are pink.
7. Add vegetables and herbs and mix well.
8. Add the retained flour mixture and sauté for 1-2 minutes.
9. Stir in the TVP, beer and stock. Stir constantly until it begins to boil.
10. Lower the heat and cover with a lid. Cook until tender. Stir occasionally.
11. Add more water or stock if you like to dilute the stew.
12. Season with salt and pepper.
13. Ladles into bowls and serve.
Calories – 229, Fat – 4 g, Fiber – 9.3 g, Protein – 17.2 g

73. Cauliflower Fried Rice

Cook time: 30 mins Servings: 4

Ingredients

- 1 lb (450 g) tofu
- 1/2 cup (150 g) peas, fresh or frozen 1 tablespoon ginger, minced
- 3 garlic cloves, minced
- 1/4 cup (30 g) green onions, sliced 1 cauliflower head, riced
- 2 carrots, diced
- 2 tablespoons sesame oil
- 3 tablespoons cashews
- 3 tablespoons soy sauce, or tamari sesame seeds, for garnish

Direction:

1. Press and drain the tofu. Then crumble it slightly in a bowl. Set aside.
2. Add oil to a wok pan and place over medium heat. Add the garlic and ginger and cook until slightly brown and fragrant, for about 1 minute. Add the tofu and stir for about 6 minutes, until golden and

well cooked. Set the tofu aside.
3. Add more oil to the pan and add the carrots. Sauté for about 2-3 minutes until tender.
4. Add the peas along with the cauliflower rice and stir until combined. Cook for about 6-8 minutes, until the cauliflower becomes tender. Add the green onions, cooked tofu, cashews and soy sauce.
5. Serve the cauliflower fried rice and garnish with the sesame seeds. Enjoy!

74. Sesame Tofu Veggies

Cook time: 30 mins Servings: 4

Ingredients
Noodles:

- 6 oz (170 g) brown rice vermicelli, or rice noodles 1/4 teaspoon red pepper flakes
- 1 teaspoon lime juice or lemon

- 1/2 teaspoon toasted sesame oil
- Sticky Sesame Tofu:
- 1 teaspoon oil
- 14 oz (400 g) firm tofu, pressed, drained and cubed 1 hot Chile, green or red
- 1/2 cup (64 g) carrots, shredded
- 2 teaspoon sesame oil
- 2 bell peppers, sliced
- 1 tablespoon cornstarch
- 1/2 cup (125 ml) water
- 1 tablespoon ginger, minced
- 1/3 cup (82 ml) soy sauce or tamari 1 cup (100 g) mixed veggies
- 5 garlic cloves, chopped
- 3 teaspoon sriracha
- 1 tablespoon orange juice
- 1/4 cup (65 ml) maple syrup
- 3 tablespoons rice vinegar
- Salt and pepper, to taste

Direction

Cilantro, toasted sesame seeds and pepper flakes, for garnish   Prepare the noodles and per the package instructions. Drain, rinse and add to a bowl. Add in the lemon juice, sesame oil, and pepper flakes and stir.

Add oil to a skillet and place over medium heat. Add the cubed tofu and cook for 5-8 minutes until slightly brown. Transfer to a bowl.

Add the peppers, sesame oil, veggies and Chile pepper to the skillet, cook for extra 4 minutes.

1. Add the ginger and garlic, cook for 3-4 minutes. Add the sauce ingredients, salt and mix well to combine. Add the crisped tofu and allow the mixture to boil for 4-5 minutes.
2. Add the cornstarch to a bowl along with water and mix well to combine. Pour the cornstarch slurry into the pan and cook until the sauce has thickened. Adjust the seasonings. Add the coconut sugar or cayenne.
3. Serve the mixture in separate bowls and add pepper flakes, sesame seeds and cilantro. Enjoy!

75. Red Curry Mac and Cheese

Cook time: 45 mins
Servings: 2
Ingredient
For the tofu:

- 1/2 teaspoon garlic powder
- 2 tablespoons soy sauce
- 1 tablespoon cooking oil
- 1/4 teaspoon black salt
- 1 lb (450 g) firm tofu, chopped
- For the cheese sauce: 2 teaspoons cornstarch
- 1 teaspoon red curry paste
- 1 cup (250 ml) almond milk
- 1 teaspoon garlic powder
- 1 1/2 cups (150 g) vegan cheddar cheese, shredded
- To assemble:
- 8 oz (225 g) macaroni, uncooked
- 3 cups (150 g) baby spinach
- 1 cup (60 g) kale
- Salt, to taste

Direction

1. Combine the pepper, salt, garlic powder, oil, and soy sauce and in a bowl. Add the tofu and coat well.

2. Preheat a pan over medium heat. Add tofu and cook until browned on all sides.

3. Add water to a pot and bring to a boil. Add the macaroni and cook until tender.

4. Combine ½ cup milk with the cornstarch. Mix well until all the cornstarch has no lumps and is fully dissolved. Add the red curry paste and dissolve.

5. Add the remaining milk to the pot placed over medium heat, and add in the red curry slurry, vegan cheese and garlic powder. Stir thoroughly until the cheese has melted and the sauce is thick and smooth.

6. Add kale along with the spinach to the cooking pot with pasta, wilt it. Drain macaroni together with the greens and return the ingredients to the pot. Pour in the tofu and cheese sauce and stir to coat well.

7. Adjust on the seasonings as desired. Serve.

76. Cauliflower Steaks

Cook time: 25 mins Servings: 4

Ingredients

- 1 cauliflower
- 2 tablespoons parsley, chopped
- 2 tablespoons pine nuts, toasted 1 tablespoon cooking oil
- 1 tablespoon golden raisins
- Salt and pepper, to taste
- ½ teaspoon lemon zest
- Romesco Sauce:
- 2 bells peppers, fresh or frozen 2 tablespoons red wine vinegar
- 3 tablespoons water
- ¼ cup (30 g) almonds, blanched
- 2 tablespoons tomato paste
- 1 teaspoon sweet paprika
- 2 garlic cloves
- ¼ cup cooked chickpeas
- ¼ cup hazelnuts, toasted
- ¼ cup (65 ml) olive oil
- Salt and pepper, to taste

Direction

1. Prepare the sauce by combining the tomato paste, red peppers, vinegar, chickpeas, water, almonds, hazelnuts, paprika, garlic, olive oil, salt and pepper in a blender, and process until smooth.
2. Preheat the oven to 400 F/200 C. Slice the cauliflower into thick steak pieces, leave the core intact.
3. Add oil to a pan, and add the cauliflower steaks. Brush the steaks with little oil and season with salt and pepper. Sear each side for 3 minutes until lightly brown.
4. Then place on the baking sheet and bake for 13-15 minutes.
5. Serve the steaks with the sauce. Top with pine nuts, lemon zest, chopped parsley, raisins. Enjoy!

77. Tempeh Burgers

Preparation time: minutes
Cooking time: minutes
Number of servings: 2
Ingredients:
- 1 package (8 ounces) tempeh

For marinade:
- 1 tablespoon sake or white wine
- ½ tablespoon grated fresh ginger
- A pinch red pepper flakes
- 2 tablespoons soy sauce or tamari
- 2 tablespoons pineapple juice
- 1 clove garlic, peeled, minced
- ¼ teaspoon white pepper

Directions:
1. Make 2 equal slices of the tempeh.
2. Add all the ingredients for marinade into a bowl and whisk well.
3. Place tempeh in it for 15 minutes. Turn once after 10 minutes of marinating.
4. Preheat the grill to medium-high temperature. Grease the grilling rack with a little oil.
5. Take out the tempeh from the marinating mixture and place on the grill. Grill for about 4 to 5 minutes on each side.

6. Serve hot over buns and toppings of your choice

Nutrition facts per serving: Without bun or toppings Calories – 225, Fat – 9 g, Total Carbohydrate – 15 g, Fiber – 9 g, Protein – 24 g

78. Butternut Squash Tofu Jambalaya

Preparation time: 15 minutes
Cooking time: minutes
Number of servings: 8
Ingredients:
- 8 cups butternut squash cubes (½ inch cubes)
- 2 tablespoons coconut oil
- 2 cloves garlic, minced
- 2 teaspoons vegan Worcestershire sauce
- 4 cups cooked brown rice
- 2 cups tomato sauce
- 4 teaspoons cayenne pepper or to taste
- 4 cups cubed, firm tofu (½ inch cubes)
- 1 large red bell pepper, diced
- 2 tomatoes, diced
- 4 tablespoons hot sauce
- 4 cups vegetable stock
- 2 teaspoons paprika or to taste
- 2 teaspoons dried oregano
- Flaky sea salt to taste

- Pepper to taste

Directions:

1. Place a soup pot over medium heat. Add oil. When the oil is heated, add garlic, tomatoes, squash and tofu and sauté for a couple of minutes.
2. Stir in the Worcestershire sauce, rice and hot sauce. Stir for 2 to 3 minutes.
3. Stir in rest of the ingredients. When it begins to boil, lower the heat and simmer until nearly dry. Stir occasionally,
4. Turn off the heat.
5. Ladle into bowls and serve.

Nutrition facts per serving:
Calories – 338, Fat – 7.5 g, Total Carbohydrate – 53 g, Protein – 17 g

79. Vegan High Protein Chili

Preparation time: 10 minutes
Cooking time: 20 minutes
Number of servings: 3
Nutrition facts per serving:

Ingredients:
- ½ can (from a 15 ounces can) kidney beans, drained
- ½ can (from a 15 ounces can) black beans or pinto beans, drained
- ½ can (from a 15 ounces can) diced tomatoes
- 2 cloves garlic, minced
- 1 small onion, chopped
- ½ bell pepper, diced
- 2 tablespoons vegetable broth
- Pepper to taste
- Salt to taste
- Red pepper flakes to taste
- Cayenne pepper to taste
- 1 tablespoon chili powder
- 1 tablespoon olive oil
- ¼ cup textured vegetable protein (TVP) mixed with ¼ cup water

Directions:
1. Place a soup pot over medium heat. Add oil. When the oil is heated, add onion, garlic and bell pepper and sauté until onion turns translucent. Stir occasionally.
2. Add tomatoes, broth and chili powder and mix well.
3. Lower the heat to low heat and simmer for 5 minutes. Add black beans and kidney beans and stir. Add more broth or water to dilute if desired. Simmer for about 15 to 20 minutes, stirring occasionally.
4. Add TVP and simmer for another t 15 – 20 minutes.
5. Ladle into bowls and serve.

Calories – 590, Fat – 7 g, Total Carbohydrate – 102 g, Fiber – 30 g, Protein – 34 g

80. Vegan Chili for Sore Muscles

Preparation time: 10 minutes
Cooking time: 25 minutes
Number of servings: 3
Ingredients:
- 1 tablespoon coconut oil
- 1 tablespoon minced garlic
- 5 medium Portobello mushrooms, stemmed, cut into cubes
- ½ jalapeño pepper, deseeded, minced
- 2 cups cooked or canned black beans, rinsed, drained
- A handful fresh cilantro, chopped, to garnish
- ½ cup lentils, rinsed
- ½ teaspoon cayenne pepper
- Pepper to taste
- 1 cup chopped bell peppers
- 1 small zucchini, trimmed, diced
- 1 tablespoon chili powder
- 2 large tomatoes, peeled, deseeded, chopped
- ½ can (from a 15 ounces can) tomato sauce

- 1 cup quinoa, rinsed
- ½ tablespoon ground cumin
- ½ tablespoon turmeric powder
- Salt to taste

Toppings:
- Avocado, chopped
- Avocado oil

Directions:
1. Cook the quinoa following the directions on the package. Set aside.
2. Place a soup pot over medium-high heat. Add oil. When the oil is heated, add bell pepper, garlic and jalapeño pepper and sauté for a couple of minutes.
3. Stir in the zucchini and mushrooms and cook until tender. Stir in the spices and cook for a few seconds until fragrant.
4. Add rest of the ingredients except quinoa and cilantro and mix well.
5. When it begins to boil, lower the heat and cover with a lid. Simmer until lentils are tender.
6. Add quinoa and mix well. Heat thoroughly.
7. Ladle into bowls. Trickle some avocado oil on top. Garnish with avocado and serve.

Calories – 344, Fat – 7 g, Total Carbohydrate – 56 g, Protein – 20 g

81. Tofu & Snow Pea Stir-Fry with Peanut Sauce

Preparation time: 15 minutes

Cooking time: 20 minutes
Number of servings: 2
Ingredients:
For peanut sauce:
- 3 tablespoons natural peanut butter
- 1 tablespoon soy sauce
- 1 teaspoon hot sauce
- 1 ½ tablespoons rice vinegar
- 1 teaspoon brown sugar

For stir fry:
- 2 teaspoons canola oil, divided
- 7 ounces extra-firm or firm tofu, pressed of excess moisture, cut into cubes
- ½ package (from a 14 ounces package) frozen pepper stir-fry vegetables (do not defrost)
- 2 cloves garlic, minced
- 1 tablespoon water or more if required
- 1 cup fresh snow peas, trimmed
- 2 tablespoons unsalted, roasted peanuts
- 2 teaspoons canola oil, divided
- 1 tablespoon finely chopped or grated ginger
- 1 cup cooked brown rice

Directions:
1. To make peanut sauce: Add all the ingredients for peanut sauce into a bowl and whisk until sugar is dissolved completely.
2. Place a nonstick skillet over medium-high heat. Add 1 teaspoon oil. When the oil is heated, add tofu and cook until brown all over. Remove onto a plate.
3. Add remaining oil into the pan. Add vegetables, garlic and ginger and stir fry for about 3 minutes.
4. Add snow peas and water and stir. Cover with a lid. Cook until snow peas are crisp as well as tender.
5. Add peanut sauce and brown tofu and mix well. Heat thoroughly.
Nutrition facts per serving: 1 ¼ cups stir fry with ½ cup brown rice
Calories – 514, Fat – 27 g, Carbohydrate – 49 g, Fiber – 7 g, Protein – 22 g

82. Crunchy Chickpea, Broccoli and Cheese Casserole

Preparation time: 30 minutes

Cooking time: 50 minutes

Number of servings: 8

Ingredients:

For vegan cheese sauce:
- 2 cups cashews, soaked in water for 9-10 hours, drained
- ½ cup nutritional yeast
- 1 cup vegetable broth or water
- 2 cups sweet potato puree
- 1 teaspoon salt or to taste
- 2 teaspoons apple cider vinegar

For casserole:
- 2 cups uncooked quinoa
- 3 cups vegetable broth
- 8 cups chopped broccoli
- 2 cups vegan cheese sauce + extra to top
- 1 teaspoon garlic powder

For crunchy chickpeas:
- 2 cans (15 ounces each) chickpeas, rinsed drained
- 2 teaspoons chili powder
- 1 tablespoon olive oil
- Salt to taste

Directions:

1. To make vegan cheese sauce: Add all the ingredients for vegan cheese sauce into a blender and blend until smooth. Use as much as required. Transfer leftovers into an airtight container and refrigerate until use. It can last for 4 days.
2. To make the crunchy chickpeas: Add chickpeas, oil, salt and chili powder into a bowl and mix well using your hands.
3. Spread it evenly, in a single layer.
4. Bake in a preheated oven at 375° F for about 25 – 30 minutes.
5. Take out the dish of chickpeas from the oven and let it cool. It will become crunchy once it is cooled.
6. Grease a large casserole dish with cooking spray.
7. Spread quinoa evenly, on the bottom of the casserole dish.
8. Add cheese sauce, garlic powder and broth into a bowl and whisk well. Taste and add salt to taste if necessary.
9. Spread cheese sauce over the quinoa. Scatter broccoli and press into the sauce.
10. Cover the dish with foil.

11. Bake in a preheated oven at 375° F for about 25 – 30 minutes.
12. Divide into plates. Scatter some chickpeas on top and serve.

Nutrition facts per serving:
Calories –421, Fat – 10 g, Carbohydrate – 66 g, Fiber – 13 g, Protein – 19.5 g

83. Teriyaki Tofu and Tempeh Casserole

Preparation time: 10 minutes
Cooking time: 40 minutes
Number of servings: 3
Ingredients:
- 4 ounces tempeh, cubed
- 5 ounces extra-firm tofu, pressed of excess moisture, cubed
- 6 ounces stir-fry vegetables, mixture of snow peas, broccoli florets and baby carrots
- 4 ounces tempeh, cubed
- 1 ½ cups cooked basmati rice
- Sesame seeds to garnish

For teriyaki sauce:
- 6 tablespoons tamari or soy sauce

- 2 tablespoons maple syrup or coconut sugar
- ¼ teaspoon garlic powder or 2 small cloves garlic, minced
- 6 tablespoons water
- ¼ teaspoon ground ginger or ½ teaspoon freshly grated ginger
- 1 tablespoon cornstarch mixed with 1 tablespoon water

Directions:

1. To make teriyaki sauce: Add all the ingredients for teriyaki sauce into a saucepan.
2. Place saucepan over medium heat and stir constantly. When it begins to boil, lower the heat and simmer for a minute or so until thick Turn off the heat.
3. Add tofu and tempeh into a bowl. Drizzle about 6-7 tablespoons of sauce over it. Toss lightly.
4. Spread it on a rimmed baking sheet lined with parchment paper.
5. Place the rack in the center of the oven.
6. Bake in a preheated oven at 400° F for 40-50 minutes. Remove the baking sheet from the oven and set aside. Reduce the temperature of the oven to 350° F.
7. Steam the vegetables following the directions on the package.
8. Add rice, steamed vegetables, tofu and tempeh into a casserole dish. Mix well.
9. Place in the oven and heat for 15 minutes.
10. Divide into bowls. Drizzle remaining sauce on top and serve garnished with sesame seeds.

Nutrition facts per serving:
Calories –654, Fat – 7.2 g, Carbohydrate – 114.4 g, Fiber – 26.7 g, Protein – 33.8 g

84. Tomato & Garlic Butter Beans

Preparation time: 15 minutes
Cooking time: 15 minutes
Number of servings: 2
Nutrition facts per serving: Without pasta
Ingredients:
- ½ tablespoon olive oil
- 1 can (14.5 ounces) unsalted petite diced tomatoes, with its liquid
- 3 ounces fresh baby spinach
- Pepper to taste
- 1 clove garlic, peeled, minced
- ½ can (from a 16 ounces can) butter beans, rinsed, drained
- ¼ teaspoon Italian seasoning
- Hot cooked pasta to serve (optional)

Directions:
1. Place a large skillet over medium-high heat. Add oil. When the oil is heated, add garlic and saute until aromatic.
2. Stir in rest of the ingredients and mix well. Heat thoroughly.
3. Serve over hot cooked pasta if desired.

Calories – 147, Fat – 4 g, Total Carbohydrate – 28 g, Fiber – 9 g, Protein – 8 g

85. Cheesy, Garlicky Pull Apart Pizza Bread

Preparation time: 20 minutes

Cooking time: 60 minutes

Number of servings: 6

Nutritional values per serving: 1 roll

Ingredients:

For pizza bread rolls:
- 1 teaspoon + 1/8 teaspoon active dry yeast
- ¾ cup warm water
- ½ tablespoon sugar
- ¾ cup whole wheat flour
- ½ tablespoon extra-virgin olive oil
- 1 cup bread flour
- ½ teaspoon salt or to taste

- ¼ teaspoon + 1/8 teaspoon baking soda

For marinara sauce:
- ½ can (from a 28 ounces can) crushed tomatoes
- 3 – 4 cloves garlic, peeled, thinly sliced
- 1/8 teaspoon red pepper flakes
- 1 teaspoon dried oregano
- ½ tablespoon extra-virgin olive oil
- Pepper or to taste
- Salt to taste
- ½ cup water

For cheesy sauce:
- ¾ cup raw cashews
- ½ cup water
- ½ teaspoon garlic powder
- 1 tablespoon nutritional yeast
- 1 teaspoon onion powder
- Salt to taste
- Pepper to taste

For brushing:
- ½ tablespoon extra-virgin olive oil
- ½ teaspoon garlic powder
- ½ tablespoons chopped fresh parsley or oregano

To assemble:
- 1 vegan Italian sausage, thinly sliced, roasted in an oven (optional)
- 4 ounces vegan mozzarella, shredded

Directions:

1. Add warm water, yeast and sugar into a bowl and stir. Set aside for 5 minutes or until frothy.

2. Add ½ cup whole wheat flour, baking soda, bread flour and salt into a mixing bowl and stir. Pour the yeast mixture into the bowl of dry ingredients and mix into dough. Add oil and mix well.

3. Knead the dough for 8 minutes until soft and supple. You can use your hands or use the dough hook attachment of the stand mixer.

4. Grease a bowl with some oil and place the dough in the bowl. Turn the dough around in the bowl.

5. Cover the bowl with plastic wrap and place in a warm area for 2 hours or until it doubles in size.

6. To make marinara sauce: Place a saucepan over medium heat. Add oil. When the oil is heated, stir in the garlic and sauté until light brown.
7. Stir in the tomatoes and water. Add rest of the ingredients and stir.
8. When it begins to boil, lower the heat and cook until thick. Remove from heat.
9. To make cheesy sauce: Add all the ingredients for cheesy sauce into a blender and blend until smooth.
10. To assemble: Grease a large baking dish with cooking spray.
11. Pour a cup of marinara sauce into the baking dish. Spread it evenly.
12. Place a layer of vegan Italian sausages in the dish. Spread the cheesy sauce over the sausages.
13. Sprinkle the mozzarella on top.
14. Place the dough on your countertop and punch it down. Divide the dough into 6 equal portions and form each into an oval shape.
15. Place the dough in the baking dish.
16. Cover the dough with a towel. Keep it in a warm area until it doubles in size.
17. For brushing: Add all the ingredients for brushing into a bowl and mix well.
18. Brush this mixture on top of the rolls.
19. Bake in a preheated oven at 350° F for 30-40 minutes or until golden brown.

Calories –364, Fat – 17.6 g, Carbohydrate – 37.2 g, Fiber – NA, Protein – 13.4 g

86. Baked BBQ Tofu with Caramelized Onions

Preparation time: 20 minutes

Cooking time: 45 minutes
Number of servings: 2
Ingredients:
- ½ block firm or extra-firm tofu, pressed of excess moisture, cut into 1 ½ inch cubes
- 1 medium onion, chopped
- 1 cup long grain rice
- ¼ cup BBQ sauce
- 1 clove garlic, chopped
- 1 teaspoon oil

Optional toppings:
- Chopped avocado
- Chopped chives
- Chopped green onion
- Chopped cilantro
- Any other toppings of your choice

Directions:
1. Spread half the BBQ sauce on the bottom of a baking dish.
2. Scatter the tofu in the dish. Spread the remaining BBQ over the tofu.

Let it sit for 15 minutes.
3. Bake in a preheated oven at 350° F for 25 minutes or until baked to the desired doneness.
4. Cook the rice following the instructions on the package.
5. Meanwhile, place a pan over medium heat. Add oil. When the oil is heated, add onion and garlic and sauté until golden brown. Stir occasionally.
6. Divide rice into 2 serving plates. Divide the tofu and place over the rice. Top with caramelized onions and optional toppings if desired.

Nutrition facts per serving:
Calories – 677, Fat – 45 g, Total Carbohydrate – 33 g, Fiber – 16 g, Protein – 51 g

87. Vegan Risotto with Sun Dried Tomatoes

Preparation time: 10 minutes
Cooking time: 30 minutes
Number of servings: 2
Ingredients:
- 3 cups vegetable broth
- 2 cloves garlic, minced
- ½ cup Arborio rice, rinsed, drained
- ¼ cup sun-dried tomatoes in oil, drained, sliced
- 1 teaspoon fresh chopped parsley
- 1 small onion, minced
- 1 ½ tablespoons olive oil

- Salt to taste
- Pepper to taste
- 2 tablespoons chopped fresh basil
- 3 tablespoons vegan parmesan cheese (optional)

Directions:
1. Place a saucepan over medium heat. Add oil. When the oil is heated, add onion and garlic and sauté until translucent.
2. Stir in the rice and cook for a few minutes until it turns opaque.
3. Add a cup of broth and mix well. Add salt and pepper to taste. Cook until nearly dry.
4. Add some more broth, tomatoes and herbs. Mix well. Cook until nearly dry.
5. Repeat adding the broth, a little at a time and cook until nearly dry each time, until rice is cooked. Stir often.
6. Garnish with vegan Parmesan cheese and serve.

Nutrition facts per serving:
Calories – 402, Fat – 13 g, Total Carbohydrate – 58 g, Fiber – 4 g, Protein – 14 g

88. Quinoa with Peas and Onion

Preparation time: 20 minutes
Cooking time: 10 minutes

Number of servings: 3
Ingredients:
- ½ cup quinoa, rinsed
- ½ tablespoon olive oil
- ¼ teaspoon salt or to taste
- 1 tablespoon chopped walnuts
- 1 cup water
- ½ small onion, chopped
- ¾ cup frozen peas
- Pepper to taste

Directions:
1. Place a saucepan over medium heat. Add water and bring to a boil.
2. Stir in the quinoa and cover with a lid. Lower the heat and cook until dry. Turn off the heat and fluff the quinoa using a fork.
3. Place a skillet over medium heat. Add oil. When the oil is heated, onions and cook until translucent.
4. Stir in the peas and heat thoroughly. Add quinoa, salt and pepper and toss well.
5. Garnish with walnuts and serve.

Nutrition facts per serving:
Calories – 174, Fat – 6 g, Total Carbohydrate – 26 g, Fiber – 4 g, Protein – 6 g

89. Swiss chard with Onions & Garlic

Preparation time:

15 minutes
Cooking time: 15 minutes
Number of servings: 3
Ingredients:
- 1 tablespoon olive oil
- 3 cloves garlic, peeled, sliced
- 1 bunch Swiss chard, coarsely chopped (8 cups)
- Pepper to taste
- Salt to taste
- 1 medium onion, chopped
- ¼ cup balsamic vinegar
- ¼ cup walnut halves, toasted

Directions:
1. Place a stock pot over medium-high heat. Add oil. When the oil is heated, add onions and sauté until translucent.
2. Stir in the garlic and cook for a few seconds until aromatic.
3. Add vinegar and scrape the bottom of the pot to remove any browned bits.
4. Add chard, salt and pepper and cook until chard wilts.
5. Garnish with walnuts and serve.

Nutrition facts per serving: 2/3 cup
Calories – 159, Fat – 10 g, Total Carbohydrate – 16 g, Fiber – 3 g, Protein – 4 g

90. Steamed Eggplants with Peanut Dressing

Preparation time: 10 minutes
Cooking time: 20 minutes
Number of servings: 2
Ingredients:
- 6 ounces baby eggplants, halved lengthwise
- ½ tablespoon soy sauce
- ½ teaspoon vegan sugar
- 1 teaspoon toasted sesame seeds
- 1 tablespoon chopped cilantro leaves, to garnish
- ½ tablespoon peanut butter
- ½ tablespoon rice vinegar
- ½ tablespoon chili oil + extra to serve
- 1 spring onion, thinly sliced
- 1 tablespoon boiling water

Directions:
1. Steam the eggplants in the steaming equipment you possess for about 15 minutes or until soft.
2. Place peanut butter in a bowl. Add boiling water into it and whisk well.
3. Add soy sauce, sugar, rice vinegar and chili oil and whisk well.
4. Place the eggplants on a serving platter. Trickle the sauce mixture over the eggplants.
5. Sprinkle sesame seeds, cilantro, spring onion on top. Drizzle some chili oil on top and serve.

Nutrition facts per serving:

Calories – 87, Fat – 5.9 g, Total Carbohydrate – 4.6 g, Fiber – 2.9 g, Protein – 2.5 g

Conclusion

Following the vegan diet has become very popular over the past decade. People switch for ethical and health reasons, and it is a great diet for people who are serious about getting healthy. But the one group of people that are still strongly judged about begin vegans are bodybuilders.

It has been a belief that the only way a person can gain muscle is by eating a bunch of lean poultry, dairy, and eggs. But the fact of the matter is, you can eat vegan and still gain muscle, and that's what this book is going to show you. Vegans come from all walks of life. They are of every nationality and every race. Being a vegan is more of a philosophy and lifestyle choice than it is an actual diet. The reasons for becoming a vegan could be to obtain better health, for environmental reasons, or due to the ethical concerns surrounding animal rights. Whatever the reasons may be for you, there is overwhelming evidence that shows how much healthier a vegan diet is for everyone, not just aspiring athletes. Some of the world's best athletes are vegan. This would not have been possible if a vegan diet had not met the needs of their bodies and increased their performance.

While many believe that a completely vegan diet is a new concept, it literally goes back almost until the dawn of human time. Everyone is familiar with the Roman Gladiators. These athletes fought wild boars, lions, and each other in arenas cheered on by thousands of people. Discoveries in recent years have shown that the diet for the majority of Gladiators was vegan. Even back then they were able to see the benefits that a vegan diet had on their performance while training and while fighting inside the arena.

A vegan diet has many health benefits. But is a vegan diet beneficial to an athlete?

Research has shown that diets that are high in foods from natural and unrefined sources play a great part in improving general health, immune systems and cardio health. With this in mind, surely it makes sense that it will improve athletic performance as well?

Printed in Great Britain
by Amazon